Growing Great Garlic

The Definitive Guide for Organic Gardeners and Small Farmers

Ron L. Engeland

Illustrated by Jim Anderson

Filaree Productions

1991

Dedicated to the late Chester "Chet" Stevenson
(1902-1990)
—May there be lots of garlic where he is now—

ISBN 0-9630850-1-8

Library of Congress Catalog Card Number: 91-76467

Published by Filaree Productions, 182 Conconully Hwy,
Okanogan, WA 98840.

Printed and bound in the U.S.A.

Illustrated by Jim Anderson
Maps by Mary Rabchuk

Typeset and Designed by Columbiana, Chesaw Route, Box
83-F, Oroville, WA 98844.

Distribution support by Glorieta School

To order directly from the publisher add $2 for shipping
and handling. Send check or money order to: Filaree
Productions, 182 Conconully Hwy, Okanogan, WA 98840.

Also distributed by Chelsea Green Publishing Co., POB 428,
White River Junction, VT 05001, 1-800-639-4099. Or in
Canada from Nimbus, 1-800-646-2879

Also available from Filaree Productions is "1995
Supplement to the book Growing Great Garlic" at $2.00 per
copy.

Printed on recycled Paper

Contents

Illustrations / Maps

Preface

Garlic has a genuine mystique some people would call an actual "power." The very sounds of the Anglo-Saxon word stir ancient, biological memories in the cells of my throat, palate, and tongue. Yet, garlic is much older than the early European culture that named it for us. The plant's simplicity is somehow fascinating and prehistoric in comparison to more complicated flowering plants. It's not difficult to imagine this plant growing at the dawn of time.

Then there is the bulb, each bulb a clone of some fantastically old mother-bulb that has grown, regrown, and multiplied its original cells for millennia. There are awesome traces of human history bundled beneath the bulb wrappers, each wrapper like a giant step through time toward the very origins of cultivated food-plants on our planet. I remember, as a younger man, the incredible discovery that plant seeds were like temporary resting places—roadside inns on an almost infinite four-dimensional highway. Now I know that bulbs, like garlic, are even more spectacular. They don't pass on their ancient memories—they **are** their ancient memories.

Unfortunately, much of what people know about garlic still prevails as old-fashioned myth and falsehood—"garlic is great for warding off vampires (and friends, too)." This book attempts to create a modern garlic-mythology through a combination of current knowledge and intelligent speculation. To be acceptable to most people, a new garlic mythology must be created within a scientific (in this instance, a botanical) framework with an ecological/evolutionary foundation, written in language understandable to lay people. Superstitions need to be replaced with meaningful history. Garlic needs to be understood as a plant, and viewed as a food rather than a generic flavoring. We desperately need to name popular garlic varieties and strains as we've long done for apples, lettuce, and squash. We need to understand that garlic has a memory (much like wine grapes) and that fine garlic (like fine wine) is an art. Some of these aspects already exist as part of the true mystique of garlic, but the mystique needs to be broadened and popularized.

I'm not a trained botanist or scientist, just a farmer in an urban culture that has long since forgotten its own agri-cultural roots, but it's worth noting that **ordinary** people were the first to cultivate garlic in the wild, and eventually to evolve it to its modern condition. Perhaps it is fitting then that an amateur and a farmer like me should attempt to describe the garlic phenomenon in lay language that any other amateur can understand.

My sincere thanks to all those special people who helped enthrall me as a garlic grower and encourage me still more to share my experiences in this book. To James Donaldson, Bob Elk, and David Granatstein; to Lurch, Hilary Green, and Bill Fujimoto; to John Swenson, Kathy Rich, Ed Spaans, Ron Bennet, and the Seed Savers' Exchange; to Dr. P.W. Simon; to Jeff McCormack and the Southern Exposure Seed Exchange; to David Stern and the New York Garlic Seed Foundation; to Lesa, Blythe, Mary, Clare, Lisa and Kurt, and all those who worked so hard and well in the fields and the warehouse; to the Hamiltons, and the employees of Hamilton Farm Equipment Center, Inc.; to Eileen Anderson, the Okanogan Highlands Community Consciousness Fund, and all those who lent their financial support; to Jim Anderson, and Mary Rabchuk for their outstanding artistic endeavors; to Thelma Achamire and all those who lent their diligent proof-reading skills; and especially to my wife, Watershine, and my family, Minot and Brianna, who help so much and sacrifice so much every year in order that we can be farmers; may you all enjoy and be empowered by the garlic mystique.

Introduction

This book is intended as a practical grower's guide, understandable and useful to amateurs, yet containing knowledge and information for experts as well. It is not a "garlic gospel," nor is it another garlic cookbook. It does answer most of the questions that no one could answer for me fifteen years ago when I began to grow garlic.

I know firsthand the frustration of not knowing and not being able to find out. Very little has ever been written about the cultivation of garlic beyond the generic gardening experience, and even less of the regional differences in climate, soil, and latitude. I wrote this book because I got tired of my own ignorance and my own unanswered questions.

The book grew almost entirely out of my own personal experiences. Whenever possible, I augmented my own knowledge with the insights of other avid growers from other regions and climates. ***Growing Great Garlic*** should quiet some of the ridiculous myths of the past; for instance, that garlic cannot be well grown in the far north. It should also point out that garlic growers still really don't know very much about the various types of garlic and their relationships to each other. In short, it should answer a lot of questions while also asking some new ones.

Growing Great Garlic is composed of three basic parts. Part I is a short history of garlic from prehistoric times to the present. Part II is a complete grower's guide from soil preparation to pre-harvest, and Part III covers harvest, storage, and marketing. The glossary in the back should prove useful to both newcomers and old-hands ***if*** garlic growers nationwide ever decide that they'd like to standardize their terminology—a decision that I would warmly welcome.

I'm still a firm believer that the field is **the** best place to gather agricultural knowledge. Much of this book was written in the garlic fields and many of my notes and journals actually have soil and dew-stained pages. If I've been successful as an author, your copy is liable to end up in the same condition as my original notes. Better yet, this book will encourage you to keep notes and records of your own.

PART I

Garlic:
Past and Present

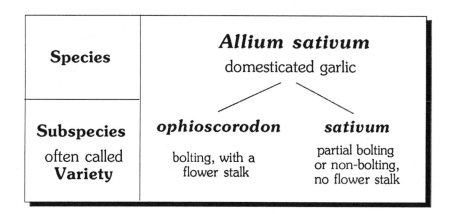

Species	*Allium sativum* domesticated garlic	
Subspecies often called **Variety**	*ophioscorodon* bolting, with a flower stalk	*sativum* partial bolting or non-bolting, no flower stalk

In Search of Respect

Bulbs are amazing plants. What could be prouder than a daffodil boldly announcing the arrival of another spring season? Its showy flowers, like most Lily Family flowers, are prized by winter-weary, indoor refugees in search of early color and new spring life. Yet, few plants are as misunderstood as bulbs. If you don't believe me, just ask a distant relative of the daffodil—garlic. If that's hard for you to visualize, it's probably because garlic doesn't fit nicely into any of the popular images we've created for plants. Consider the following.

Garlic is not commonly referred to as a food, a spice, or an herb—it's just garlic. A lot of Americans apparently relish it because commercial farmers produced nearly one pound of bulbs for every person in the nation in 1980, yet we still had to import even more than that to satisfy demand. Odd then that so few Americans admit that they like it. Garlic seems to invoke its own special psychology so that many people have an easier time eating it than they do talking about it.

Part of the negative garlic psychology is certainly associated with the old and widely held belief that garlic makes human bodies stink. The simple truth is that the pervasive odor in question is the result of individual body chemistry. Watershine (my wife) and I know people who eat garlic daily without ever smelling of garlic, and we know people whose stench drives us out of the room if they eat one clove per month. The vast majority of garlic eaters experience only the mild and temporary discomfort of "garlic breath"—which can be easily masked—but the offenses of a few odiferous individuals continue to cast a dark shadow on garlic as a food.

Aside from the taste, most people are at a complete loss to describe the garlic plant and bulb. It looks like the plant has a normal stem—don't all plants? Well, yes, but on garlic it's not the green, leafy portion that everyone continues to call a stem. The "true stem" is entirely below ground and almost flat as a pancake.

Another oddity, garlic plants begin growth in the late fall when normal plants are dying or already dead. In fact, the garlic clove never dies, and leaf growth begins inside the clove long before the clove is even planted. Cloves are actually swollen leaves, but no one would dream of calling them leaves. Botanists call them "fleshy scales" (which sounds a bit like bloated fish skins). Technically, the cloves are small bulbs within a bulb, but no one, not even botanists, ever refer to cloves as bulbs, and no one knows why cloves are called cloves.

Few people know how or when cloves are formed either. A common misconception, even among garlic growers, is that a large, solid bulb grows and then divides into cloves right before harvest. Actually, tiny vegetative buds occur on the surface of the true stem at the base of the inner leaves. Some of the buds are fertile (another strange term, since they never actually get fertilized). Specialized leaves swell into cloves around each fertile bud in midspring in order to nourish and protect the bud through its period of rest and during its early growth. Notice that I said "period of rest." Most people assume garlic bulbs lie "dormant" until they're planted, but according to botanists, they only "rest."

Then there is the famous (or infamous) garlic flavor which most people have never actually tasted because the softneck garlics commonly grown are so "hot" that the flavor is overwhelmed. You haven't tasted real garlic flavor until you've tasted an "ophio" garlic.

Ophio garlics are the half-wild garlics that still produce a flower stalk. Unfortunately, the flowers are very un-*Allium*-like. They're not at all bold and showy. They often wither on the bud before they can even open, and they're so small and inconspicuous that no sane gardener would call these flowering plants, even though they are—technically.

In short, garlic is an amazingly simple yet highly deceptive plant. What you see depends a lot on whether you're talking to a botanist, a farmer, a produce buyer, or a layperson as well as which part of the country you are from (all of which only determines the specific brand of confusion and misnomers you'll be dealing with).

Generally speaking, garlic has been relegated to the cultural status of a sub-food (i.e. "less than a food"), at least in the highly visible public eye. Despite its wide and varied uses (not to mention a history—which started long before humans even invented history), garlic is not a favorite conversation piece. You might well show off your daffodils to a neighbor, but you probably keep the garlic in a corner of the garden where it won't attract attention and comments. (Oh, so you *like* garlic!) Professional botanists have also largely avoided garlic on the grounds that it was (and is) not a major food crop or ornamental crop (i.e. not a cash crop).

Well, ten thousand years of outrageous misfortune are enough. Despite stems that aren't really stems, flower stalks without noticeable flowers, cloves that are really leaves (or bulbs or fleshy scales—whatever), fertile buds that are never fertilized (so how did they get fertile?), and a plant that never dies no matter how old it gets, it's time for garlic to be shown some respect.

Modern Garlic

Garlic (*Allium sativum*) ranks as the second most important *Allium* crop in the world (behind only onions). The species is divided into two subspecies (often called varieties) whose botanical Latin names are a mouthful—ophioscorodon, and sativum. I will use the terms "ophio" and "softneck" when referring to the two subspecies. Ophio garlics, which may also be called "topsetting" or "hardneck" garlics, evolved directly from the wild garlic known as *Allium longicuspis*. Softneck garlic, which may also be called "Artichoke," or sometimes "Italian" or "Silverskin" garlic, evolved later from the ophio garlics. Softneck garlics are the most commonly grown garlics in the world, but it all began with ophio garlics.

Ophio Garlic ——————————————————————

Ophio garlics are quite similar to wild garlic in character and flavor. All of them produce woody flower stalks (sometimes called "false seedstalks" because no fertile flowers or true seed are produced) rising from one to six feet above the leafy portion of the plant in late spring. The flower stalks are topped by a large capsule called an "umbel" that encloses small aerial cloves known as "bulbils." The flower stalk, technically known as a "scape," twists somewhat athletically into either a loose curl or a tight coil shortly after it emerges, but later loses its curl and stands up straight as bulbing begins. As it stands up, the stalk becomes woody rather than succulent. The stalk and umbel are the most obvious features that distinguish ophio garlics from softneck garlics, and they are the reason some people call them "topsetters" or "serpent garlics."

Ophio garlics normally produce a single circle of cloves around the central woody stalk. Close examination of the bulb will reveal that the circle of cloves is actually divided (nearly in half) by a single skin. Technically, this means the circle is composed of two "layers" of cloves opposing each other. The two layers indicate the plant had only two fertile leaves with buds in the leaf axils, each bud forming a clove.

Ophio garlics typically produce between four and fourteen cloves per bulb, but the type most commonly grown in North America has between six and ten easy peeling cloves. Most experts admit ophio garlics have far more flavor than the more domesticated softneck garlics that evolved from them. The combination of few but large cloves, high, half-wild flavor, and easily removed clove skins make ophio garlics extremely popular in gourmet restaurants. In recent years, they've also become more widely recognized among consumers as well. Perhaps their only disadvantage is their short period of storage (quite similar to that of wild garlic). This is especially true of the specific type known as "Rocamboles." They want to begin root growth in the early fall and commonly begin to do so, at least by October, if humidities are over approximately sixty-five percent. This largely limits their popular use to a short season (basically August through November), and they are often called "fresh market, gourmet garlics" for that reason.

Confusion over the term "Rocambole" has existed for centuries, primarily because some writers apply the same generic term to another *Allium* species (*A. scorodoprasum*), which is similar to garlic but has far fewer cloves that are usually non-uniform in size and shape, a dark violet bulb wrapper, and a much shorter flower stalk. *Allium scorodoprasum* is edible but is not known as a cultivated plant. Because of the application of the generic term "Rocambole" to two different species, some people erroneously believe that Rocamboles are not true garlics. Currently, the term "Rocambole" is only applied to true garlic, and specifically to that group of ophio garlics which have tightly coiled flower stalks (i.e. not simply curved or arched).

Despite the belief that ophio garlics evolved before subspecies *sativum* garlics, no specific mention of garlic with topsets or coiled flower stalks is made in the ancient literature. Not until about five hundred years ago did ophio garlics gain enough popularity in the Mediterranean region that specific references finally occur. My own suspicion is that ophio garlics had long been grown and cherished in certain localities and in certain traditional families and ethnic groups, but were far less popular than softneck garlics because of their much shorter storage and lower productivity per unit of area. It's not difficult to imagine that most people considered ophio garlics to be wild specifically because of their coiled flower stalks and the fact that only small bulbs were usually produced unless someone cut off the flower stalk shortly after its appearance.

The specific lack of reference in the ancient literature suggests strongly that the process of evolution/human selection had already produced many softneck (subspecies *sativum*) garlic strains as early as five thousand or six thousand years ago. These cultigens are more productive per acre and longer storing; in short, more domesticated. Subspecies *sativum* garlics probably remained the popularized garlic of high civilizations (and, therefore, literature) until advances in human culture allowed the relative luxury of large scale production of the ophio garlics, which required more labor, more land, and more skill to produce, while storing only a few months.

Softneck Garlic

The appearance of *A. sativum* subspecies *sativum* must have marked a great turning point in the usefulness and popularity of garlic. So-called "Artichoke" garlics are large-bulbed and vigorous despite their sometimes pale-green leaf color. They are generally coarse-skinned, not always beautiful, but highly productive in a wide range of climates and soils. In some climates (such as Germany), they still often produce topsets, but in most climates they produce only a few large bulbils out the side of the false stem a few inches above the bulb. These bulbils may even appear as small, odd-shaped cloves inside the bulb wrappers at the very top of the bulb. Some strains produce no bulbils at all. Whenever energy is not diverted to flower stalk and bulbil production, these garlics are capable of very large bulb size. In addition, they typically store longer than ophio garlics; for many farmers, that means greater volume can be produced with less fear of sprouting and rotting before it can be sold.

Artichoke garlics compensate biologically for their lack of flower stalk and bulbil production by producing more cloves per bulb. Most types have between three and five fertile leaves (or clove layers) in a sort of swirl vaguely reminiscent of an Artichoke plant. Total cloves per bulb may range from eight to forty. These garlics generally lack the high flavor of ophio garlics, tending instead to taste either very hot or very mild. (In general, cold winter climates make all garlics taste hotter.) Yet, Artichoke garlics are highly suitable for the popular uses to which garlic is most often applied by civilized people—namely, as flavoring, and (in more recent times) as a flavoring in dehydrated, powdered form, but seldom as a raw vegetable. For instance, more than two-thirds of the commercial garlic in California is dehydrated.

Like their ophio ancestors, softneck garlics can be differentiated into several distinct varieties, but the thousands of strains so long in cultivation and popular use make the varietal distinctions even harder to detail than they are in ophio garlics. In fact, many growers would claim that softneck garlics are less stable than ophios and more likely to display a wide range of environmental responses. For instance, when some of the strains do bolt and form flower stalks (or partial stalks—see "partial bolting" in glossary), they may form ophioscorodon-type bulbs with two clove layers.

Elephant Garlic

Let me clear up one common misconception right from the start. Elephant Garlic is **not** a true garlic. It is a leek, *Allium ampeloprasum*, though it's sometimes erroneously listed in seed catalogues as *Allium sativum* "Giganteum" (among other names). Leeks may be divided into three basic varieties or horticultural groups—the Leek Group, the Kurrat Group, and the Great-Headed Garlic Group. The latter was popularized in America by the Nichols Garden Seed Company in Oregon which began selling it under the name "Elephant garlic" several decades ago. (According to John Swenson, the name "Elephant Garlic" was first used by Luther Burbank in 1919.)* This plant is also called "Oriental Garlic" in some regions, probably because the French name is "Ail d'orient".

While Elephant Garlic is a leek, it produces very large, garlic-like cloves with a very mild garlic flavor (though the taste sharpens in cold winter climates). The plant has not been studied in detail and there are no known official collections of Elephant garlic in the world, but the plant is cultivated in the U.S.A., Greece, India, Chile, and the Netherlands, among others. In some northern climates, such as the Netherlands, Elephant garlic commonly forms only large, undivided rounds (much larger than garlic rounds) which are used much like pearl onions. In other regions, four to six-cloved bulbs commonly weigh up to one pound each.

Elephant garlic produces a solid seedstalk which does

---

* Personal letter to the author from John Swenson, 1991.

not always curl or curve. The flower cluster is very large and typically *Allium* in nature, but the flowers seldom open widely and are not very fertile; thus, propagation is primarily by cloves. The spathe splits open and falls off the flower cluster (the garlic spathe usually remains intact even if it splits open). Elephant garlic also forms "corms" off the side and bottom of the main bulb. Corms have very tough shells (like nuts) with a sharp point at the top end. The corms can be planted, but must be soaked in water for several days to soften the hard exterior surface.

Elephant garlic's flower stalk should be cut off as soon as it forms in order to help size up the bulbs which are commonly harvested with or just ahead of Artichoke garlics, as soon as the leaves begin to brown out. The neck of the plant never hardens or turns woody enough to allow the huge bulbs to be pulled from the ground without tearing the tops off.

Subspecies Summary

The two basic subspecies of garlic differ primarily in their reproductive habits. The earlier evolved ophioscorodons are primarily bulbil producers and, at least originally did not produce large bulbs unless bulbil production was halted by flower stalk removal. Softnecks are primarily clove producers and bubil production is normally insignificant. The two subspecies do not differ significantly in soil and cultural requirements, although most softnecks are harvested slightly earlier than ophioscorodons (Silverskins are usually an exception). However, subspecies *ophioscorodon* definitely requires more management and skill in order to produce large, high-quality bulbs suitable for commercial marketing, and most subspecies *sativum* seem more adaptable to a wide range of climates.

Garlic Varieties

Most modern experts now recognize two varieties of cultivated garlic—variety *sativum* and variety *ophioscorodon*. While we are not taxonomic authorities, we believe the general public would be well served by elevating these to subspecies status. The fact that these two basic kinds of garlic differ in their reproductive tendencies convinces us that they differ more on a species level than on a varietal level, and subspecies means literally "almost a species." (We view ophio garlics primarily as bulbil producers, and sativum garlics primarily as clove producers.) Our choice of subspecies ranking corresponds with the work of the Russian, Kuznetsov (whose work will be described in the next chapter). Finally, we believe that it serves little purpose for sativum and ophioscorodon to be varieties when we can expect every garlic grower we know to answer "Silverskin" or "Artichoke," rather than "sativum," when asked the question, "What variety of garlic do you grow?"

Professionals have wrestled with the problem of garlic varieties for over one hundred years and basically succeeded in creating a very fine mess with very little agreement. A few highly respected individuals still refuse to recognize any distinctions at all within the species, *Allium sativum*. Most at least recognize the difference between ophio and softneck garlics, but none seem willing to go beyond that level of classification.

We believe strongly that the lack of official recognition of basic types of garlic entails a great disservice to garlic growers (who have little choice but to take matters into their own hands) and to the public (which is not to blame for its near total ignorance concerning garlic). There is certainly no motivation for consumers or gardeners to experiment with varying forms or to seek out new tastes and qualities as long as garlic remains generic garlic.

Imagine, if you will, what would happen if American seed companies sent out annual catalogues that offered generic lettuce, beans, and peas, with no recognition of the distinctions between bush, pole, and shell beans, lima and fava beans, head lettuce and leaf lettuce, field peas or sugar peas, not to mention the hundreds of named strains of each. Gardening would not only be dull, it would be difficult. Yet, such has been the fate accorded garlic by professional researchers despite the ironic fact that garlic is one of the oldest cultivated food plants known to civilized culture.

Our current theory is that we should be able to identify distinct garlic varieties (both ophio and softneck) corresponding to the three basic eco-geographic regions where garlic evolved as a semi-domesticated food plant. These regions will be fully described in the next chapter on history, but they basically correspond to eastern Europe, central Asia, and eastern Asia (see Figure 8 on page 47). This would entail a minimum of six garlic varieties.

Varietal descriptions cannot be static; instead, they must describe a range of character whose specific features (or traits) vary both by environment (i.e. annual and geographic variations) and by degree of domestication. Varieties will undoubtedly overlap in character so that some varieties may be difficult to distinguish in certain climates. We believe that varietal character can be described by recording specific traits as bell-shaped curves with areas of high and low probability. By overlaying the ranges of variation experienced by different growers in different climates in different years, we should be able to verify and complete useful varietal descriptions within three to five years.

The varietal descriptions and drawings of four tentative varieties that appear at the end of this chapter are probably too specific since data from growers in other regions is just beginning to come back to us. They are, however, accurate representations of the most commonly occurring features of four distinct types of garlic as grown at Filaree Farm in north central Washington state.

Bear in mind that when small, non-vigorous plants and bulbs are grown, the varietal characters tend to disappear until only the most obvious distinctions between ophio and softneck garlics remain. The larger the plants and bulbs, the easier it becomes to recognize and describe the sometime subtle differences. The size and number of individual plant parts is obviously relative; for instance, a small bulbil capsule on a large and vigorous plant is significant while a small plant probably can't be expected to produce anything but a small bulbil capsule.

In other words, it's difficult to judge the character of any garlic strain based on only one year of growth. We suggest painting a composite picture over a minimum two to three year period. We can probably always expect to find some strains that exhibit characters of more than one variety simply because garlic has been domesticated, mutated, and selected for so many centuries. In those cases, growers will have to use their best judgement.

We're currently trading information with other garlic growers in varying climatic regions, including micro-regions within Okanogan County and macro-regions, such as the maritime Pacific Northwest, the desert Southwest, the Midwest, and the Northeast. Eventually, that should give us information about the specific responses of certain key garlic strains (which we call our "standards of reference") to climates, soils, longitudes, and altitudes.

It takes several years to establish a collection of garlics in a location and "settle them in" (acclimate them to local conditions), and several more years for the grower to establish a routine that ensures good data collection. We know a lot of good garlic growers who just aren't good record keepers, so it takes time to initially identify the right people for the task, more time to actually accumulate meaningful data, and more time still to analyze the data. At this point, the national network is still very young and most of our descriptive information and speculative classification is based primarily on our own observations here at Filaree Farm.

The point to be made is that generic descriptions and

public recognition of six or eight basic varieties of garlic will greatly enhance the public image of garlic even if the varietal descriptions are not one hundred percent accurate and acceptable to professional botanists. The standardization and popular usage of a few varietal names by growers and distributors are the first step in simplifying the current maze of localized vernacular. These can elevate garlic in the public eye to the status of a "civilized" food plant with name-brand recognition. Individual strain names will still be useful in certain markets, but since the same identical strain may have four or five invented local names in the United States, it is the broader varietal names that will allow recognition of the basic character regardless of whether a strain is sold in California or Chicago.

Similar public recognition on a subspecies level would be helpful, but we view names like "*ophioscorodon*" and "*sativum*" as far too esoteric for use by the general public. At the other end of the spectrum, terms such as "hardneck" and "softneck" are probably too generic to be really meaningful. We hope that our proposed varietal names, such as "Rocambole" and "Silverskin," will offer both the charisma and meaning necessary for them to be useful to both growers and buyers.

Our tentative classification of cultivated garlic into varieties is as follows:

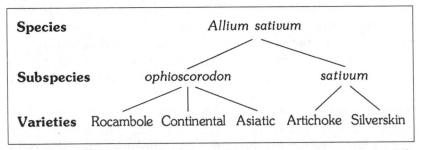

Species	*Allium sativum*				
Subspecies	*ophioscorodon*			*sativum*	
Varieties	Rocambole	Continental	Asiatic	Artichoke	Silverskin

Artichoke garlics appear to be the most commonly grown garlics in North America, but the Silverskin variety may run a close second. A few authorities consider the term "Silverskin" to be a "linguistic artifact" every bit as useless as generic terms such as "Italian Red." Silverskins are, nevertheless, quite popular in climatic regions that bring out their best character, such as the western

United States, France, and northern Italy. They are certainly very distinctive as grown at Filaree Farm, and they're widely recognized by growers and buyers in most of the United States.

In most climates Silverskins rarely form any bulbils. They also tend to have more total cloves per bulb than standard Artichoke garlics. These two factors suggest to some people that Silverskins may be the most highly domesticated form of cultivated garlic, and they probably were selected from mutations of standard Artichoke strains. This variety is apparently planted in springtime more than any other type of garlic, but it's also planted from October through January in many regions. Silverskins are called "Italian" garlics in some commercial garlic areas of the deep south, and sometimes "Egyptian" garlic in California and the southwest.

Rocamboles appear to be the most commonly grown ophio garlics in North America. While long popular with some gardeners, they've begun to make quite a splash in specialty markets and gourmet restaurants in the last twenty years due to their exceptional flavor. Unfortunately, they're harder to grow and generally shorter storing than other garlic varieties.

Continental garlics are still relatively rare in North America, but we think they have a bright future. They share most of the qualities of Rocamboles, yet appear to store longer. They may turn out to be slightly less productive than Rocamboles.

We have yet to positively identify a garlic strain of the Asiatic variety, but we do have some top prospects. In general, we've had a hard time collecting samples of East Asian garlics, and we still don't have a wide sampling.

To be widely accepted these varietal names are going to have to prove more useful than the many generic terms currently bandied about. For instance, many softneck garlic strains have gained the names "Italian Reds" or "Italian Purples" because so many of them were brought to America by Italian immigrants. In general, despite the fact garlic was widely used by peasants in northern Europe, the people from such countries as Russia, Poland, and Germany never achieved the reputation of "garlic lovers" the way the Italians did. Certainly, the Romans loved garlic and Roman soldiers scattered it across the known world. Today, the myth continues. The truth, however, is that just as many garlic strains came to America from other European nations. In fact, the name "Italian" has often been applied to garlic strains that certainly never grew in Italy. Most professionals now consider the terms "Italian Red" and "Italian Purple" to be horticulturally useless despite a number of popular American garlics so named. If the terms are still widely used, it is as a result of myth more than place of origin, and the terms tell us almost nothing about the fundamental character of garlic strains.

Ironically, most ophio garlics in the United States came here from central and northern European nations such as Germany, Poland, and Russia. Others came from Greece, France and Spain as well, but no ophio garlics from Italy every gained distinction here. Nevertheless, ophio garlics are grown in Italy, sometimes by the name "Italian Somona." In general, ophio garlics usually have the terms "red" or "pink" as part of the strain name in Europe and (with the notable exception of the term "Italian Red") this often distinguishes them from softneck garlics. French ophio garlics are commonly termed "Rose" or "Violace" garlics, or just plain "Early Pink," "Early Red," or "Rosy" garlics, whereas softneck garlic is known as "common garlic" (or *ail de ordinnaire*). Common garlic is often called "white" or "Blanc" garlic in France.

Likewise, Spanish softneck garlic may be "Ajo vulgar" (or common garlic), but ophio garlic is "Ajo rojo" (red garlic). There are also popular individual strains, such as Banjolis.

Among Americans the terms "red" or "white" garlics are still sometimes used, but professionals generally avoid them. The terms are very confusing to novices and consumers because many white-bulbed garlics actually have very red cloves; likewise, so-called "red garlic" may have almost no bulb color and very light brown cloves. The unfortunate truth is that many American consumers still think all garlic (wild or otherwise) originated in Italy and is the softneck type. Only strongly ethnic groups are likely to distinguish between ophio and softneck garlics, or between German, Russian, Spanish, or Greek origins. Very few Americans know the difference between softneck and woody-stemmed garlics, and the botanical Latin names (such as *ophioscorodon*) are virtually unknown.

The nearly total lack of American knowledge about garlic varieties is perhaps best exemplified by the vast majority of American seed catalogues. They typically may offer five or six types of lettuce or potatoes, but just one generic garlic with no name or description. Hopefully, that's one thing that readers of this book will help to change.

[Note: the varietal descriptions that follow are generally accurate, but there are always exceptions to the rules. We continue to find a few strains that have apparently been locally adapted over a period of many years to conditions not normally conducive to their varietal type; for instance, a Rocamoble that performs well in a mild winter, maritime climate, or a Silverskin that performs well in Montana. Several people tell us they have even "trained" garlic strains over long periods by careful annual selection of individual plants.]

Subspecies *ophioscorodon*
Rocambole Variety—typical

Subspecies: *ophioscorodon*
Variety: Rocambole
Leaf:
    Color: deep green or blue green
    Erectness: moderately spreading (i.e. fan-shaped)
Bulbil:
    Presence: almost always unless stressed by heat or grown in mild winter climate.
    Location: umbel at tip of flower stalk
    Size and Number: generally ten to forty, usually large or huge, but varying from small to huge.
    Maturity: mid (i.e. after Artichoke but before Continental)
Flower Stalk:
    Height: moderate (three to five feet when uncoiled)
    Shape: distinctively coiled in one to three tight loops
Spathe Color: usually whitish (rarely yellow-white)
Beak Length: moderately long
Umbel Size: large to very large
Bulb:
    Shape: fairly symmetrical, flat globe shaped, some irregularity
    Size: (in fertile soil) 2" to 2.75"
Bulb Skins:
    Color: off-white with widely varying amounts and degrees of light to moderate purple blush or blushed streaks
    Texture: moderately coarse (but finer in poorer soil)
Number of Fertile Leaves: two—rarely three
Cloves:
    Number per Bulb: three to fourteen, but six to eleven most common
    Shape: plump round if well grown, but tall, narrow, wedge-shaped when many cloves per bulb
    Color: basically brownish with widely varying amounts of red-purple blush, always dull colored
    Skins: extremely easy to peel
    Doubled Cloves: quite common in most strains, but rare in a few
Bulb Maturity: mid (i.e. after Artichokes)

Natural Dormancy: short (three to four months)

Storage: three to four months, but six to occasionally eight months possible if well grown and cured.

Flavor: probably best of all garlics when well grown and locally adapted

Soil and Climate: generally perform best in cold winter climates and require fertile soil to size bulbs. Generally fussy about soil and may develop yellow leaf tips easily in poor or unbalanced soils or during cool wet periods.

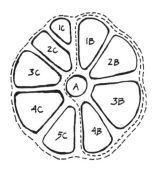

Rocambole
typical

The schematic drawing shows the typical clove arrangement in Rocambole variety. "A" is the woody flower stalk (a specialized leaf). "B" and "C" are two separate clove layers, each surrounded by its own bulb wrapper (thin broken lines) which is the lower portion of a foliage leaf. The cloves in each layer are numbered. Each clove is a swollen leaf sheath formed specifically to protect and nourish the bud that it surrounds. Foliage leaves with buds (and eventually cloves) in the leaf axil are called "fertile leaves." Additional bulb wrappers (not shown) would surround the entire bulb, but since they have no cloves in the leaf axils they are called "infertile leaves."
Note: drawings are not all to the same scale.

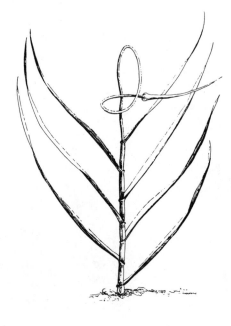

Subspecies
ophioscorodon
Continental Variety
Type 1

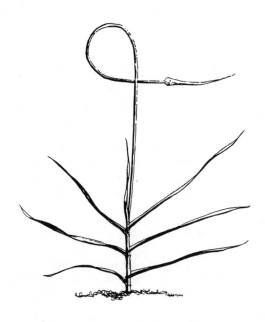

Subspecies
ophioscorodon
Continental Variety
Type 2

[Note: currently Type 2 seems distinct from Type 1, but may only be the result of small, non-vigorous plants]

Subspecies: *ophioscorodon*
Variety: Continental
Leaf: wide spaced on false stalk—plants taller than Rocamboles
    Color: pale to deep green
    Erectness: wide spreading to moderately spreading on Type 2; spreading near false stalk but then tall (to four feet) on Type 1.
Bulbil:
    Presence: almost always unless heat stressed
    Location: umbel at tip of flower stalk
    Size and Number: numerous and very tiny
    Maturity: late (i.e. after Rocamboles)
Flower Stalk:
    Height: very tall (five to seven feet when uncurled)
    Shape: two types; broad sweeping 270 degree curl in Type 2, or wild irregularly shaped coils in Type 1
Spathe Color: yellowish—but sometimes whitish
Beak Length: long
Umbel Size: small in most, but can approach size of Rocambole in some strains.
Bulb:
    Shape: highly symmetrical, globe shaped
    Size: (in fertile soil) 1.5" to 2.5"
Bulb Skins:
    Color: two types; porcelain or purple streaked
    Texture: fine to slightly coarse
Number of Fertile Leaves: two in most strains, but some tend to have three
Cloves:
    Number per Bulb: 3 to 10, but 4 to 6 most common in porcelain type; 8 to 12 in purple type
    Shape: plump round, but tallish at top with short, stout tail in porcelain type; taller, narrower in purple type
    Color: buff brown background often streaked heavily on top half with dull but striking purple; varying degrees of pink or red-pink blush, vivid compared to Rocamboles
    Skins: harder to peel than Rocamboles, but easier than softnecks

Doubled cloves: very rare
Bulb Maturity: late (i.e. after Artichokes and Rocamboles and about the same time as Silverskins)
Natural Dormancy: moderate (four to five months)
Storage: moderate to long (four to eight months)
Flavor: higher than softnecks, but not quite as high as Rocamboles; mild after harvest, but often hotter after curing.
Soil and Climate: may do best in cold winter climates and require good soil to size bulbs.

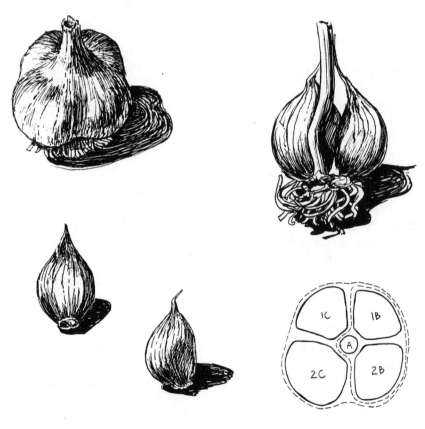

This example of the Continental Variety has two clove layers and four total cloves. Note the elongated clove skins at the tips of the cloves.

Continental
typical

Subspecies *sativum*
Artichoke Variety—typical

Subspecies: *sativum*
Variety: Artichoke
Leaves:
  Color: average to slightly pale green, occasionally dark green
  Erectness: fairly upright to slightly spreading
Bulbils:
  Presence: highly variable by cultigen and climate. A few rarely produce bulbils; most have bulbils in 10% to 40% of the population.
  Location: lower one third of stem or in the top of the bulb, but on topsets in some climates
  Size and Number: large to huge, generally only one to five
  Maturity: early (before all other garlics)
Flower Stalk: generally nonexistent, but appears in some climates or in some years on some individual plants
Bulb:
  Shape: varies from flat to thick flat or flat globe
  Size (in fertile soil): 2.25" to 3"
Bulb Skins:
  Color: off-white to dirty white or yellow-white; sometimes light purple blush
  Texture: coarse to very coarse
Number of Fertile Leaves: range of two to eight (rarely more), but three to five are most common
Cloves:
  Number per Bulb: range of twelve to twenty-four, but most types average twelve to eighteen.
  Shape: plump, squarish to high topped for outer cloves; tall, thin and narrow to small round for innermost cloves
  Color: generally milky white with small subtle amounts of pink or brown blush at tip or base, but some kinds have pink blush throughout and/or reddish partial stripes.
  Skins: adhere tightly on most cultigens.
  Doubled Cloves: very rare, but a few cultigens occasionally produce large outer cloves that subdivide into several smaller cloves, each with their own skin.

Bulb Maturity: early to medium early
Natural Dormancy: medium to long (four to five
months)
Storage: six to nine months
Flavor: varies from very mild to very hot depending on
strain and climate.
Soil and Climate: appear to be most widely adaptable
garlics.

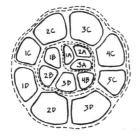

This example has four clove
layers (i.e. four fertile leaves),
and fifteen total cloves.

Artichoke typical

Subspecies *sativum*
Siverskin Variety—typical

Subspecies: *sativum*
Variety: Silverskin
Leaf:
  Color: often pale green, sometimes average green
  Erectness: generally very upright, but sometimes
      drooping at ends
  Bulbil: rare in most climates, but on topsets when they
      appear (generally as the result of stress or cold
      winters)
Bulb:
  Shape: varies from tallish globe to elliptical
  Size: varies by climate; 1.5" to 2.25" in many regions,
      but larger possible
Bulb Skins:
  Color: white when well grown; occasionally off-white
      with copper veins
  Texture: fine and smooth
Number of Fertile Leaves: three to twelve possible, but
      commonly five to eight
Cloves:
  Number per Bulb: eight to forty, but either eight to
      twelve or eighteen to twenty-four most common
      depending on type. May produce secondary
      cloves on bottom of bulb.
  Shape: usually tallish concave (cylinder or spindle) but
      may be flat wide
  Color: either white or pink blushed
  Skins: adhere very tightly
  Doubled Cloves: extremely rare in some climates, but
      more common in others. Many strains produce
      large outer cloves that subdivide into several
      smaller cloves, each with their own clove skins
Bulb Maturity: late (after all others most years)
Natural Dormancy: Long (four to six months)
Storage: long to very long (six to twelve months)
Flavor: varies from very mild to very hot
Soil and Climate: appear to perform best in mild winter
      climates with good soils and long season.

Silverskin
typical

This example has five clove layers (i.e. five fertile leaves), and fifteen total cloves. Outer cloves "1E" and/or "2E" are likely in some strains to subdivide into two or three smaller cloves.

The History of Garlic

Among Amerindians there is an old saying that goes something like this:

"It is not wise to choose a chief until you have looked seven generations into the Earth."

There is great wisdom in that adage. As regards our current purpose, it suggests that while almost anyone can grow garlic, the best growers will be those that also understand garlic. True understanding is more than skin deep; it entails various experiences which broaden our perspectives. Garlic cannot grow without roots, and good garlic growers cannot truly understand the plant they are nurturing without historical perspective.

Wild Garlic: An Ancestral Plant

Garlic has been cultivated for many thousands of years, perhaps being one of the earliest wild plants tended by humans. Nearly all experts now agree that the original hearth place of garlic was in south-central Asia. In the rugged ravines and steep hillsides of a series of mountain ranges extending from the remote Tien Shan in the east, through the Pamir-Alai Range and on to the Kopet Dagh in the west, approximately one hundred fifty species of Alliums are found. (see figures 1 & 2)

Though Candolle names the place of origin of the garlic plant simply as "the Kirgiz desert region of Siberia,"* the original "garlic crescent" probably ran along the modern Soviet border with China, Afghanistan, and Iran, in the

---

* Candolle, Alphonse de, 1908, *The Origins of Cultivated Plants*, D. Appleton Co., New York.

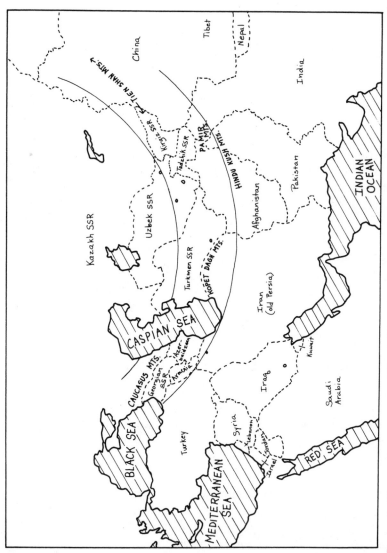

Figure 1. The modern nations and republics of south-central Asia, and the approximate region of the extended garlic crescent including the southern Caucasus. The primary hearthplace of wild garlic is considered by many to be the rugged foothills of the Tien Shan, Pamir, and Kopet Dagh mountain ranges.

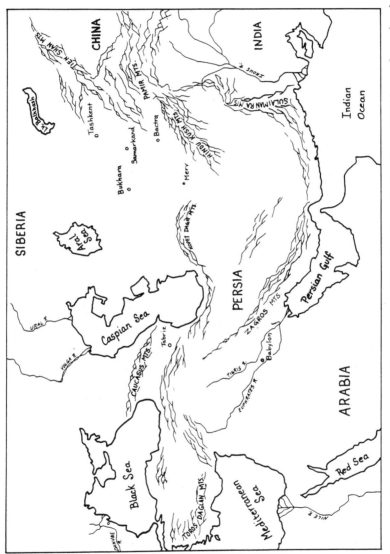

Figure 2. Mountain ranges of south-central Asia. The locations of the cities of Bukhara, Samarkand, and Tashkent are shown as points of reference for the garlic crescent.

southern portions of the modern Soviet republics of Kirgiz, Tadzhik, Uzbek, and Turkmen. Nearby cities, such as Tashkent, Samarkand and Bukhara, have very ancient histories yet remain remote and mysterious to Westerners even today. Most of the modern inhabitants are still Turkic speaking peoples of the Sunni Muslim faith who are descendants of ancient nomadic tribes people.

In 1875, a researcher named Regel* discussed the wild garlic he named *Allium longicuspis*. The so-called "long cusp" referred to tall filaments on either side of the flower anthers that were visibly extended from the perianth whenever flowers fully developed. By contrast, the flowers of cultivated garlic (*Allium sativum*) usually wither as buds and rarely open at all; if they do manage to open, they are usually infertile. Only with diligent searching have fertile plants of cultivated garlic been produced in small numbers by experts in Germany, Japan, and the United States.

Regel's description of a wild *A. longicuspis* corresponded somewhat with occasional references in old, non-scientific literature to a wild garlic capable of producing true garlic seed. Since the cultivated garlics of the western world had never been known to produce true seed, Regel's description stirred a certain amount of excitement in Europe and North America, all the more so because Westerners were denied easy access to the wild garlic in its natural habitat.

However, some twentieth century horticultural experts, seemed to consider *A. longicuspis* a wild ancestral garlic rather than a true modern species. Not until the 1980's were several dozen of the *A. longicuspis* specimens finally introduced to North America in quantity and planted out for observation in cultivated environments. The specimens proved to be virtually indistinguishable from the modern, topsetting ophio garlic as far as farmers and gardeners were concerned, but research experts did find a few distinctions.

Currently, some modern experts, such as Dr. P.W.

---

* referenced in Jones, Henry A., and Louis K. Mann, 1963, *Onions and Their Allies: Botany, Cultivation and Utilization*, Interscience Publishers, Inc., New York.

Simon, supervisory research geneticist for the USDA Agricultural Research Service at the University of Wisconsin's Department of Horticulture, generally agree that *A. longicuspis* deserves ranking as a separate species of garlic.* Others believe *A. sativum ophioscorodon* and *A. longicuspis* should be merged into a single group; however, the designation of "longicuspis" for modern wild garlic is still very useful to some experts. Therefore, some people suggest "longicuspis" could be classified as *A. sativum*, but with a subspecies rank equal to (but separate from) the subspecies *ophioscorodon* and *sativum*. The latter course may eventually be chosen, but, at the current time, *A. longicuspis* is still classified as a separate species because of its botanical distinctions and its apparently distinct geographical pattern of occurrence. The classification as a separate species probably will not change as long as the distinction remains useful to experts.

Historically, it now seems quite possible that wild *A. longicuspis* (and other early food plants) were cultivated by semi-nomadic hunter-gatherers more than ten thousand years ago. If that is the case, then the truly wild species may only be a relic of a long, lost age of human pre-civilization. Ten millennia of evolution accentuated by even minor human interference could have obliterated the original character of the plant long before modern times.

It is very clear now that grains were widely grown and abundant in mountain villages southwest of the garlic crescent four thousand years before the rise of Sumer in Mesopotamia, so cultivated plants were already a common commodity. Most historians, archaeologists, and paleontologists now believe that the entire Middle East was a thriving, sprawling center of early human culture comprised of many dozens of small empires and proto-cities long before the rise of the first known Mesopotamian cultures about five thousand years ago. (see Fig. 3)

The evidence and artifacts from the recently discovered ruins of the city-state of Ebla in modern Syria include detailed written records and maps (over fifteen thousand

---

* personal letter to the author from Dr. P.W. Simon, 1991

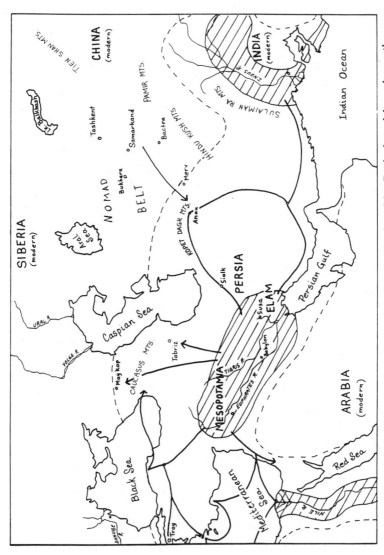

Figure 3. Cross-hatched areas show the early centers of urban life. Dark dotted line shows the area of early villages. The solid lines show early trade routes. Cities of Bukhara, Samarkand, and Tashkent not yet built, but frequented by nomadic tribes.

clay tablets) that clearly name and locate over five thousand named places within a one-half million square-mile region. The tablets also document heavy trade and long distance travel at a time when we thought the first great civilizations were still being born. In fact, one-quarter million Eblans lived on the plains surrounding the city with thirty thousand inhabitants, fifty-foot tall walls, and an academy for scribes that taught at least two languages as prerequisites to higher studies. Included here are the oldest known written references to biblical patriarchs such as Abraham and David.

The surprising documentation of long-distance trade and travel many years before the rise of Sumer makes it almost certain that *A. longicuspis* had a long and colorful history. We know that the region of the garlic crescent was a major trading route between the peoples of China and the Mediterranean throughout all of written history (see Fig. 4). It served as a natural bridge that had to be followed in order to pass south of the great Siberian marshes and Tien Shan Mountains, yet north of the great mountains of the Hindu Kush. The only other route was far to the south through India. We also know that prior to the age of civilized trade the huge region, historically known as Turkestan*, was dominated by various nomadic cultures—such as the Avars, and later the Iranian Complex sometimes referred to as Aryans.

That the region was probably well travelled in prehistoric times is perhaps substantiated by its astoundingly busy history during the last two thousand years. The region was conquered and heavily influenced by Turks, Arabs, Persians, Mongols, Chinese, and even Greeks. The Macedonian, Alexander the Great, made his capital at Samarkand. The same city was visited by Marco Polo, Genghis Khan, and virtually every other traveller, trader, and conqueror of the past ten millennia (see Fig. 5, 6, & 7).

---

* Historic Turkestan became offically known as "Soviet Central Asia" in the late 1920s when the Soviet Republics were formed along ethnic and geographic lines. Old Turkestan included all of the current Soviet Republics of Turkmen, Uzbek, Tadzhik, and Kirgiz, as well as southern Kazakh.

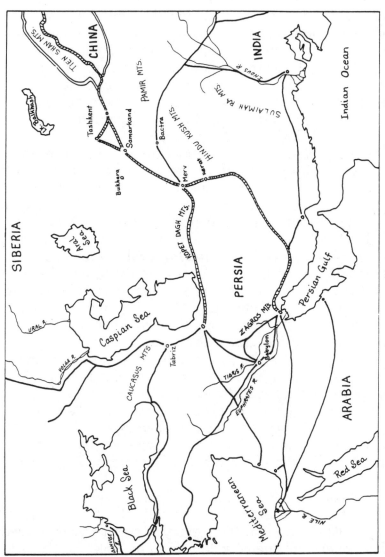

Figure 4. The famous Silk Route (cross-hatched double line) was officially established in 128 B.C., but was a well travelled pathway for much earlier nomads and hunter-gatherers as well. It ran from central Persia to China, directly through the garlic crescent in northeast Persia.

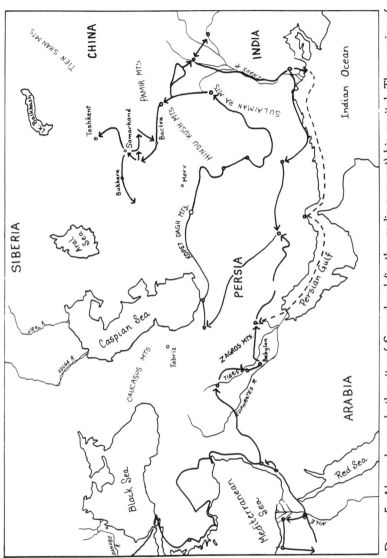

Figure 5. Alexander made the city of Samarkand (in the garlic crescent) his capitol. The empire of Alexander extended from Greece to India in the 4th century B.C.

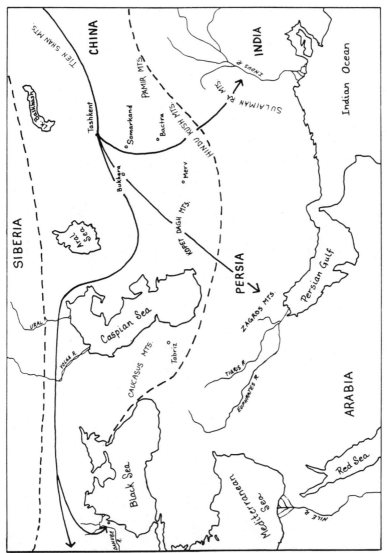

Figure 6. Major routes of invasion by early barbarians in 5th and 6th centuries A.D. Southern routes used by the Huns; northern route by the Blue Celestial Turks. The broken lines show the northern and southern limits of the nomad belt.

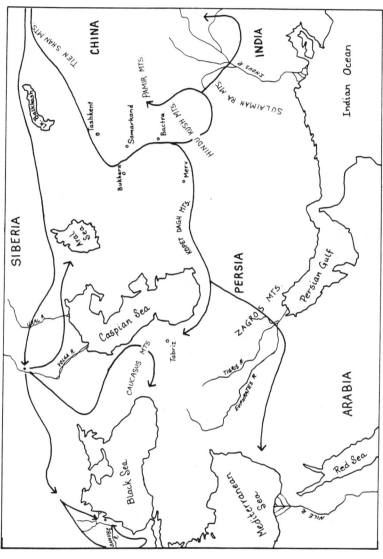

Figure 7. The Mongol Hordes travelled directly through the garlic crescent as had conquerors, traders, and travellers for millenia.

Surely indigenous tribes people and pre-historic hunter-gatherers not only collected wild garlic for immediate use but also carried it with them wherever they journeyed. Garlic's light weight and its easy storage for periods of at least several months would have made it a convenient and popular companion even when nomadic peoples carried only scant baggage. Garlic may have been considered at least a semi-valuable herb because of its great potency, small size, easy storage and, eventually, its ease of culture. Very early on, it had obvious value not only as a flavoring for a wide array of otherwise wild and bitter foods, but also as a preservative of both meats and vegetables. Garlic not only prolongs the storage life of meat because of its anti-microbial properties, but also masks the flavor of rancid meat and fish.

There is also justified speculation that garlic was used ritualistically, as well as medicinally, by early hunter-gatherers. Apparently, the layers of skins were believed to be symbolic of the layered heavens surrounding the planets of the solar system (i.e. the cloves).

In short, wild garlic may have been very widely dispersed in very early times and could easily have been passed by nomadic tribes to more southern villagers, and from there to Egypt, the Mediterranean, and India within a few millennia of the last Ice Age. That it was well known by all the early civilized cultures is well documented. Specific mention of garlic occurs many times in the oldest known written language, Sanskrit, dating back more than five thousand years. Egyptian clay models of garlic more than five thousand years old were found in pre-dynastic cemeteries, and actual bulbs were found in five thousand year old tombs. There was even a reputed labor strike by slaves building the great pyramid at Cheops 5,750 years ago because work-masters reduced the daily ration of garlic. Fifteen pounds of garlic was said to be the price of a healthy slave. Garlic was also grown in the famous Hanging Gardens of Babylon where a shipment of 395,000 bushels was reputedly received. Chinese scholars prized the virtues of this little bulb as both food and medicine. The Romans actually referred to Hebrew people as "the stinking ones" because they used garlic, and Egyptians were called "onion eaters" or "the garlic eaters."

Obviously, the plant considered a staple nearly six thousand years ago in a civilization as far removed from the birthplace of garlic as is Egypt, must already have had an ancient history of its own.

Primary Centers of Distribution ─────────

The likelihood of very early dispersion from its original hearth place probably greatly extends the geographic region of garlic's early evolution. The extended garlic crescent (see map page 32) reaches into China and Mongolia in the east, and westward to the Caucasus Mountains (west of the Caspian Sea). Some scholars consider not only the Caucasus regions of the Georgian, Armenian, and Azerbaidzhani SSR, but also the southern Ukraine (to the north) and Turkey (to the southwest) as a broad primary center of dispersion.

The Russian Kuznetsov[1] recognized two distinct biological types of topsetting ophioscorodon garlics from the general Caucasus region. He called them the Caucasian and East Caucasian groups. His third group, called Central Asian, corresponded to the original hearth place of garlic east of the Caspian Sea. Later, in 1964, the Russian Komissarov[2] reported that the large "Mediterranean Group" (corresponding to the two Caucasian Groups of Kuznetsov) had given rise to numerous non-bolting garlics (softneck) after centuries of cultivation and domestication in a broad region that also included the Balkan states and the Crimea. These regions, encircling the entire Black Sea, are believed to be the more recent evolutionary sources of most of the Mediterranean and European garlics that were eventually carried to North America, South America, and Africa. (see Fig. 8, page 47)

The specific Caucasus region is a natural bridge of dispersion northward into Russia, the Ukraine, and eastern Europe, as well as south to the shores of the

[1]Komissarov, V.A., translated by John F. Swenson, 1964, "On the Evolution of Cultivated Garlic, *A. sativum* L., Proceedings of Timirjazov Agricultural Academy, No. 4: pp 70-73.
[2]ibid.

Mediterranean or southwest through Turkey to southeastern Europe. The Caucasus has an intriguing history of its own. In the ancient Hellenistic world, it was divided into Colchis (in the west) and Iberia (in the east). Colchis is the land where Jason and the Argonauts searched for the mythical Golden Fleece. Though the Georgian people are a high and ancient culture in their own right, the southern Caucasus was influenced by the Greeks and Romans, not to mention the Persian and Byzantine Empires. Like historic Turkestan, the Caucasus was ravaged by Mongols in the 13th century, and again by Tamerlane in the 14th century.

Prior to written history, the Caucasus served as a major route for travellers between the Don and Volga River valleys in the north (the gateway to the steppes of southeastern Europe and cultures such as the Cossacks) and the early pre-historic mountain villages above the plains of the Middle East. Tabriz would eventually be established as the center of this hub of travel and trade. The Caucasus differs from Turkestan as an historical crossroads only in its wider ranging climates and stronger Mediterranean and European influences. Even if it was not the hearth place of wild *A. longicuspis*, it must be considered one of the primary centers of distribution for most of the western world.

Garlic is known to have been introduced to eastern China by traders via India and Afghanistan during the Han Dynasty about one century before the birth of Christ. On the other hand, garlic is supposedly mentioned in the Calendar of Hsia about 2,000 years earlier. Legends even maintain that native wild garlic already existed prior to that in Chekiang Province on the east coast of China just below Shanghai. The legend claims that the wild garlic "crossed with the introduced garlic" so only one type exists today. This is yet another suggestion that in ancient times garlic was able to produce true seed from fertile flowers. Candolle also points out that the Chinese symbol for garlic is written by a single sign which usually denotes "a long known and even a wild species." Certainly China served as a major area of domestication despite the fact that few of these garlics ever reached the western world.

Climatic Effects

The climate of the garlic crescent is harsh and continental. Summers are very hot, soils dry, and the direct sunlight quite intense. Winters are long and severe. This general condition has been fairly constant for at least the last six thousand years despite minor fluctuations in worldwide climates.

Wild garlic typically matured in late spring, then lay dormant in the dry soil until the arrival of fall moisture and cooler temperatures. The plant was well equipped to survive great deficiencies of moisture because its small but succulent bulb was protected by tough, dry, and persistent scales (known as bulb wrappers) as well as thick inner clove skins with specialized membranes that kept moisture in and climatic extremes out.

The natural period of rest in mountainous regions was actually very short compared to other vegetables whose seed lay dormant until spring. Root growth on garlic cloves began only two to three months after maturation and dieback of the mother plant. Sprouting and leaf growth commonly, though not always, occurred in fall. Young leaves were soon buried and insulated in deep snow, and no damage was done as long as the garlic had deep roots prior to winter.

The most vigorous vegetative growth occurred in the early spring when moisture was abundant from snowmelt, and growth proceeded quite rapidly so that bulbing could begin as soon as hot days and long hours of sunlight occurred in May or June. Growth and maturation were often complete by the arrival of the summer solstice when days were scorching hot and soil moisture nearly nonexistent except on north slopes or in hidden ravines.

Such wild garlic was clearly unaccustomed to pampering. The soils it frequented were sandy and dry, rich in minerals no doubt, but very poor in tilth and nutrients. Rainwater, often as not, was a luxury. The environment of the last six thousand years was a far cry from the rich garden soil, nitrogen fertilizer, and irrigation water of the twentieth century.

The movement of garlic eastward from the garlic crescent into China and Mongolia probably did not entail very many cultivated soils or much human management; in fact, those soils and climates were generally even more extreme and harsh than in south-central Asia. Nevertheless, garlic is still found today in regions as hostile and far north as Buryat where permafrost exists in some locations and the influence of Siberian cold is constant.

The early centers of Chinese civilization were also far to the north. It is, therefore, interesting to note that Shanghai (on the south coast of China) lies at the same latitude as Cairo, yet commonly experiences winter temperatures nearly thirty degrees colder than Cairo. Consider the extreme cold in the interior regions of northern and western China where ancient garlic was probably first introduced. In general, the Chinese Asian climate must be considered similar to the climate of south central Asia although certainly more extreme in some regions.

Quite the opposite climatic conditions awaited garlic in the Mediterranean type climates to the south and west of the garlic crescent. The climate of the eastern Mediterranean tends to be wet in winter and droughty in summer. But while the summer climate has surprising similarities with that of south central Asia, the moderating effects of the Mediterranean Sea prevent extreme winter cold and allow year round vegetative growth in some areas.

And, finally, continental Europe usually experienced year round rain. Winters were wet and cold but far less bitter than those of Asia. Summer heat was much more moderate than in either Asia or the Mediterranean, and soil moisture was usually plentiful.

These are the three basic climatic regions which much of our modern garlic evolved in as an early domesticated plant. I call them "Mediterranean, Continental, and Asiatic." Each appears to have played an important role in the development of distinctive bulb and plant characteristics.

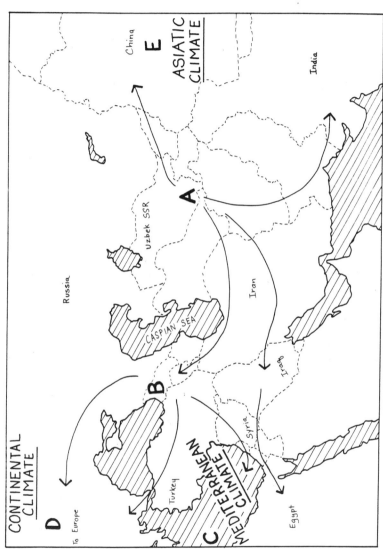

Figure 8. A=hearthplace of wild garlic in Soviet Asia; B=Caucasus region; A & B=primary centers of dispersion; C, D, & E=basic geographic-climatic regions resulting in distinguishable groups.

PART II

Cultural
Requirements

Sites and Soils

Garlic is highly adaptable. Almost anyone in North America can grow garlic—but those growers with ideal soils and climates do have an advantage. Most ophio garlics (topsetting/bolting) require a cold winter to ensure high vigor and quality. Only a particular group of ophios, which I call "Southern Continental," perform better in the southern United States than in northern regions. Many Artichoke garlics also perform well in northern climates but, unlike ophios, often perform equally well in southern climates. Silverskins are perhaps the fussiest, yet we've seen high quality Silverskins grown in every corner of the United States.

Ideal Environment

Generally speaking, most garlics appreciate winter cold because it somehow invigorates the plant and brings out the best quality. It also tends to make garlic taste hotter—not always an advantage. Below-ground roots and bulbs are seldom damaged by subzero temperatures and frozen soil **unless** the soil freezes very suddenly and very deeply. Snow cover usually insulates soil against rapid deep-freezes, but a heavy mulch is highly recommended in cold winter regions sometimes shy of snow. Cold temperatures can damage plants if significant above-ground growth occurs before winter. The idea is to plant about four to six weeks before the ground normally freezes; that allows good root development but not top-growth prior to winter. Maritime and southern growers can plant as late as December or January in most years since above-ground leaf growth can proceed all winter. In test plantings as early as August at Filaree Farm in north central Washington, we achieved as much as twelve inches of top growth prior to winter and found no winter killed plants the following spring despite sub-zero temperatures and no more than four inches of snow cover at any one time.

Good spring and summer sunlight is a prerequisite for quality. Warm to moderately hot days and long hours of sunlight coupled with moderately cool nights are ideal. Too much summer heat (temperatures over 95 degrees Fahrenheit) for more than a few days can cause early maturity and reduced bulb size. Too many cool, cloudy days can reduce vigor, but, more importantly, cool weather late in the season interferes with bulbing. Wet climates are not necessarily a problem. It depends on when and how much moisture occurs at any one time. Plentiful moisture in early spring is OK, but lots of rain in late spring and early summer can be disastrous. Garlic needs heat to begin bulbing (mid to late May in north central Washington), and it needs relatively dry weather conditions to permit harvest and curing (July or August). Thus, semi-arid, northern climates with moderate fall and spring rains are ideal.

Soils are also important to quality. Garlic probably evolved in poor soils with general deficiencies of moisture and nutrients. Many people (including the author) would claim that small bulbs well-grown in poor soil still produce the best tasting, best keeping garlic bulbs. But, small bulbs don't sell well in America.

Sandy loams with moderately high levels of soil organic matter (3% to 4%) are good for market garlic. Heavier loamy soils or soils with more than 5% organic matter can produce much larger bulbs if they are well-drained, but bulbs may not store as long and they may have less color. They may also be difficult to clean. In general, dark and/or heavy soils tend to produce bulbs with dirty and/or stained bulb wrappers unless soils are fairly dry at harvest.

Sandy soils are difficult to manage because they dry out so rapidly. Sandy soils with a high silt content may turn hard and tight when they dry out. The addition of organic matter to sandy soils raises the moisture holding capacity and the level of stored nutrients, as well as providing a looser structure that allows plants to breathe.

Clay soils are undoubtedly the hardest soils in every respect. They tend to drain slowly (thus, bulbs are too wet). They tend to be very tight when dry (thus, bulbs can't breathe). They tend to discolor bulb wrappers and cling tenaciously to both roots and wrappers despite furious attempts at cleaning.

The ideal environment for many garlics is one with moderately cold winters, good snow cover, adequate fall and spring moisture, a warm and dry June and July with good direct sunlight and low humidity, and a light sandy loam with moderate organic matter and good drainage. We think that moderate elevations of two thousand to four thousand feet can also be helpful because they ensure cooler summer nights and they seldom experience excessively high summer temperatures.

Artichoke garlics have very similar requirements to ophio garlics, but they don't seem to need the winter cold as much. They're more adaptable to maritime climates, although high summer humidity or rain can cause mold and disease problems and make it very difficult to cure the garlic after harvest. The near Mediterranean-type climate of central California seems to be ideal for many Artichoke strains while others seem better adapted to cold and less tolerant of heat.

We haven't noticed that southern exposures or frost pockets significantly affect garlic production as long as soils are well drained. Leaf tips can die back after spring frost, or whole leaves can wilt and die after hard frosts; still, garlic is more frost hardy than typical garden plants.

Regionally, the western United States is better suited to garlic production then the east because it tends to have lighter, better drained soils, less summer rain and humidity, and more intense, direct summer sun. This certainly does not imply that good garlic can't be grown in the eastern United States. It just means that Westerners tend to have some built in advantages that make the whole process less worrisome and slightly less prone to pitfalls (such as heavy downpours just before harvest). A very vigorous and active cadre of small garlic growers has been created in New York and New England during the last decade, due in part to the formation of the New York Garlic Seed Foundation by David Stern of Rose, New York. A less organized network of garlic growers now exists in Minnesota and Missouri, and a Virginia company, named Southern Exposure Seed Exchange, offers more garlic cultigens than any other small seed company in America that we're currently aware of.

In summary, some sites and climates are better than others, but good experienced growers can probably do well growing garlic in almost any state. If you're in doubt, try testing several different types of garlic to see how they perform at your site. Keep good records, and increase production gradually so that you have a chance to learn about handling and timing before you suddenly have one ton (i.e. twenty thousand bulbs) of garlic to deal with.

Scale of Production

"How much?" is a question at least as important as "where, when, and how?" The temptation is always to plant too much too soon.

Many prospective garlic growers are lured by the high price per pound often paid to expert growers for high quality, gourmet garlic. The high price is the direct result of superior quality and that usually means "small-scale, handcrafted, organically grown." As the volume of production increases, quality is always going to deteriorate— and so is the price per pound.

Most small-scale, organic garlic growers are part time farmers who plant between fifty and two hundred pounds of cloves per year on one-tenth to one-fourth acre. They harvest between three hundred and fifteen hundred pounds of bulbs and supplement their annual incomes with $500 to $3,000 in gross sales. Many such growers market their crop through local farmers markets or small food co-ops. These growers probably produce a majority of all fresh market garlic in America.

Small-scale growers can certainly achieve a level of quality that is unattainable by large scale growers, but they work very hard to do so. Every task, from planting to bulb cleaning, is performed entirely by hand, and this is basically the kind of work that most Americans describe as tedious and menial. It takes a special character and attitude—in addition to certain skills—to achieve consistency in this sort of "labor of love."

Fifteen hundred pounds of fresh garlic is a lot of bulbs for a part time farmer to handle. It requires an old barn or a fairly large outbuilding for curing and storage. Very few growers can increase their scale of production beyond about fifteen hundred pounds without hiring labor, mechanizing, or investing money in drying sheds. We know a lot of people who've tried to produce five thousand or ten thousand pounds using the same methods as for fifteen hundred pounds—and been thoroughly overwhelmed in the effort.

Fifteen hundred to ten thousand pounds of fresh garlic can still be hand crafted and organically grown, but only experienced growers should attempt it. Labor will have to be hired. At least some tasks will probably have to be mechanized (such as weeding). Money will likely have to be invested to insure an adequate drying facility and special expertise will be required in order to sell the product—probably through distributors or brokers.

Not many mid-sized garlic growers currently operate in America, but we feel this is a scale of production with a lot of potential, particularly if several such growers market cooperatively. The potential problems are enormous, and we believe strongly that growers should work their way cautiously into this scale of production rather than jumping into it aggressively. Whenever production surpasses approximately one thousand pounds, growers quickly (and, sometimes, painfully) discover that, while anyone can grow garlic, only a few can grow superior quality garlic. The timing of each operation becomes more critical as scale of production increases; for instance, over mature garlic can result from a harvest that takes two weeks to complete.

Large scale garlic production (over ten thousand pounds) almost always involves mechanization of planting, weeding, and harvesting. Skilled growers can produce good garlic, but seldom gourmet quality; thus, the price per pound falls rather drastically. Most large scale growers produce some or all of their crop for processing so that damaged, over mature, and stained bulbs remain usable.

Our very strong recommendation is to start small—one hundred pounds of planting stock is probably far too much if you've never grown garlic. Even if you've grown a few pounds in your garden for many years, the problems involved in the sheer handling of thousands of bulbs can be surprisingly overwhelming. Grow your way to success gradually, learn as you grow, and expand your growing skills before you try to expand your markets.

Soil Preparation

No single aspect of garlic production is overlooked and ignored as often as soil preparation. If you're gardening garlic for your own use then almost any good garden soil will suffice, but if you're growing for commercial sales—at any scale, large or small—then soil preparation is often the deciding factor that determines success or failure.

I've spent fifteen years helping other small farmers get started as garlic growers. I always try to strongly emphasize soil preparation, and the response I get most often is "No problem, I've got this piece of virgin ground that's never had anything grown in it," or "This place is ideal; it was farmed until ten years ago and hasn't had a thing done to it since then."

I cringe noticeably at those kind of responses. They tell me that I'm dealing with an inexperienced grower—one who never learned the basics about soil, and probably isn't going to bother to learn the basics about garlic. Of course, that's to be expected in a culture that spent much of the last fifty years researching techniques that would allow American farmers to sidestep and shortcut the basics as often as possible.

The "basics" begin in the soil or, perhaps more accurately, with the fundamental realization that dirt and soil are not the same. Soils are alive. Dirt is potential soil waiting to be born. Particularly in the western United States with its thin mantle of fragile topsoil painstakingly woven a few centimeters per year, the actual distance separating dirt and soil can be erased in less than one season of intensive crop growth. A single tilling of the soil can bury an entire century of topsoil and dilute it so severely that commercial crop production of a vegetable like garlic is doomed before it's actually planted.

Would-be garlic growers would do well to face a few simple facts. If garlic is grown for commercial sale, then bulb size and appearance are going to be at least as important as taste and keeping quality. Americans like big vegetables because large size translates subconsciously into vigor, robustness, and health. Never mind the more subtle truths of the matter. Bigger isn't just better; it's a necessity if you're depending on consumers to buy your product.

Garlic probably evolved in poor soils, but those soils won't grow large bulbs or clean and beautiful bulbs. Good garden type soils will. Whether you plant one-tenth of an acre or ten acres, you will have larger, more attractive bulbs if you plant in moderately fertile, garden type soils.

Now, remember that piece of virgin land that's never had anything grown in it? It may be natural but it's also probably poor. Virgin land in the western United States is often low in organic matter for one thing (probably less that 1.5%) because western soils and climates are mostly arid or semi-arid—they can't support much natural plant growth, so soil building is a very long and arduous proposition.

One solution is to speed up the natural process of soil building by growing green manure crops. It's fairly easy if you can irrigate the ground but very tricky and generally a lengthier process if you're a dryland farmer. Easterners, too, can benefit from green manure crops since they face the problem of rapid decay and leaching of nutrients that require very regular replacement. Any process that incorporates lush, green plant matter into the soil is going to add nutrients and provide the raw materials necessary either to sustain or initiate a healthy population of microorganisms. You won't find them in dirt or in subsoil—not in appreciable quantities. You can even purchase them and apply them to your soil, but they won't survive if organic matter levels are too low. On the other hand, most of them appear and multiply almost magically once organic matter is supplied.

Of course, warm temperatures and moisture are also prerequisites. Decay occurs best when conditions are optimal. No decay at all (or, worse yet, rot) may occur when soils are too wet, too dry, too cold, etc.

I begin soil preparation for garlic a minimum one year before planting. Two years is better. No wonder then so many would-be garlic growers get a great notion in September, plant in October, and find themselves out of the garlic business less than one year later.

Grass sods build topsoil faster than any other natural process, but grass sods are horrible environments for garlic. Therefore, we often plant land to grass or grass-clover sods *one and a half years before* we plant garlic. Fall is the best time to sow seed, but early spring is not bad—it's just difficult to work soil in early spring because it's usually wet and cold.

My favorite sod-building, cover crop is a rye grain/red clover/fescue combination planted in mid-September. The rye grain germinates almost immediately. It greens the field before winter and protects the soil from the ravages of subzero temperatures, surprisingly hot winter sun, and bitter winds. In the spring the rye acts as a nurse crop supplying shelter for the grass and clover, but it needs to be mowed in mid-spring to keep it from growing too tall and crowding out the grass and clover.

We irrigate and mow the grass/clover cover all summer, finally turning in the accumulated organic matter (roots, thatch, and top growth) in early September. That leaves time to plant winter rye again in mid-September—this time all by itself. The rye is then turned under in April. It's followed by spring oats, and then two successive crops of buckwheat during warm weather before final preparation of garlic planting in October.

If one full year of irrigated sod followed by four quick green manure crops sounds like a lot of work just to grow one garlic crop—it is. But then we grow large-bulbed, intensively planted garlic, and our goal is two-fold—great garlic, and soil that's richer after we harvest garlic than it was before we first decided to plant the garlic two years earlier. We have to achieve both goals if we expect to keep growing great garlic for many years.

Of course, there are always variables. (You knew there'd be a catch.) Actual requirements will vary by region and by soil. If soil has a hardpan, for instance, then subsoiling is required. Subsoiling breaks up the hardpan, aerates the soil, and allows drainage, yet does not bury valuable topsoil deep in the ground. Garlic requires a well drained soil, so sub-irrigated ground may be a poor choice, or it may require drainage tiles.

Likewise, clay soils require special attention since they retain water and tighten up as they dry out. I've seen good garlic grown in raised (or almost elevated) beds so that winter meltoff and spring rains filled the trenches without drowning and rotting the garlic bulbs, but special management, extra preparation and labor were necessary.

Some soils have specific nutrient deficiencies that require fertilizers. A good soil test in combination with a leaf analysis is often the only way to determine extreme nutrient deficiencies. Garlic fends well for itself in nutrient poor soils (when compared to common garden vegetables) but may benefit from added nitrogen.

Far more common than extreme nutrient deficiencies are simple imbalances, but those take us into grey shadowy areas where no two experts recommend the same solution. If imbalances are suspected, I recommend a good basic soil building program for at least two years. Soil organic matter and soil microorganisms cure far more nutrient imbalances than do fertilizers (in fact, the latter often create serious imbalances while they're curing specific deficiencies). If you intend to fertilize, then I recommend organic fertilizers—raw materials that require decay by soil microorganisms in order to release their blend of nutrients via the natural soil process. There are lots of shortcuts to this process, but most of them also shorten the viable life span of the farm.

Manures

Do cropped soils need animal manures? I didn't used to think so, but I've tempered my views after fourteen years of garlic production. All natural ecosystems (which I believe we should try to mimic in some fashion) involve the recycling of both plant and animal wastes in the process of soil building. Manure from large mammals may occur in only small volumes, but it is present. The bulk of animal waste actually comes from soil microorganisms—not their actual wastes so much as their own decaying bodies—but the entire soil process can certainly be enhanced by the addition of some animal manure provided it is *well* managed.

At Filaree Farm we often compost rabbit manure directly into our garlic fields the summer before an October planting. I like rabbit manure because it's not too high in nitrogen and it's weed free. Horse manure would be my second choice, provided it's not mixed with a sawdust bedding material, but most such animal manures *will* contain weed seeds. These materials are best composted before application to the soil. If they are sheet composted directly into the fields then time should be allowed for initial decay and re-establishment of balanced nutrient availability, as well as irrigation/rainfall during weather warm enough to germinate the weed seeds. I like to apply horse or cow manure in late spring or early summer (even if it's several years old and well aged) so I can spend the summer "growing the weeds out of it." In other words, I take advantage of the weed seeds by using them as green manure crops.

Chicken manure is often the easiest manure to locate, load, and haul, but it requires careful management. It's one of the "hottest" manures (nitrogen rich), and it can burn garlic severely unless it's incorporated into the soil well in advance of planting (absolute minimum sixty days).

Manures are a double-edged sword. They greatly enhance the tilth and structure of soil no matter how old they are, and they often provide needed nutrients, but they have to be managed as to time of application and amount. Too much of a good manure can damage both crop and soil the same way that too much of a synthetic fertilizer can upset the intricate web of balances in a healthy soil.

Other Soil Amendments

Soil amendments are of two basic types—raw organic matter, or multi-faceted nutrient sources in mostly unrefined form (e.g. kelp meal). Both require some basic cautions.

Many new converts to organic agriculture decide they have an acute soil organic matter deficiency and set out to solve the problem in a single weekend by incorporating many tons of sawdust, sludge, leaves, animal manure, or old straw into their soil. Many of them end up in trouble.

Sawdust can make a good mulch, but it also contains turpins, resins, and pitches that are highly toxic to plants when present in large amounts. Sawdust is also very high in cellulose and low in nitrogen; thus, it will require a great deal of added nitrogen in order to decay. It will steal nitrogen from crop plants if there isn't enough of the nutrient available. Sawdust can also retain large volumes of water and keep garlic bulbs constantly wet. I don't highly recommend sawdust as a mulch, and I suggest never incorporating it into the soil unless you intend to delay crop production for at least two years—time for the sawdust to decay without directly affecting crop plants.

Animal manures, despite obvious benefits if composted or sheet composted, generally make poor mulching materials in my experience primarily because they retain so much water they rob moisture from the soil (and plant roots) while, ironically, rotting the plant at the soil surface. I've seen crops die from lack of moisture despite weekly irrigation because a manure mulch prevented the water from entering the soil profile. This can happen whenever structural differences (e.g. between manure and soil) prevent capillary transfer between surfaces. The result may be water that puddles at the soil surface and keeps the manure mulch soggy wet.

Straw can also be a mixed blessing when incorporated into the soil. First, it's almost pure cellulose that needs nitrogen in order to decay. Secondly, whether used as a soil amendment or a mulch, it's liable to contain some very noxious weed seeds. In the latter case, mulching is not much different from actual seeding of the weed into your soil.

Old straw can be very useful. We sometimes mulch garlic with old, chopped, wheat straw. In a particularly poor soil we may also incorporate the same straw (or better yet, fresh alfalfa hay) into the ground in order to build soil organic matter levels rapidly. In either case, we make sure the straw is "clean" (i.e. weed free). When used as a soil amendment we do it well in advance of crop planting and add a nitrogen source, such as blood meal, to aid the decay process.

Sewage sludge, more than any other possible soil amendment, is like a surprise package. Never apply sewage sludge without a thorough chemical and structural analysis beforehand.

Weed Control

This is perhaps the most overlooked aspect of soil preparation and yet the vast majority of vegetable farmers in America will tell you that weed control is their number one problem/expense. Indeed, far more money is spent on herbicides than on insecticides in American agriculture—both field-scale and garden-scale.

We've never applied an herbicide in seventeen years of farming. It just doesn't make good sense to us to waste a vital source of nutrients and soil building material while risking short and/or long term contamination of the soil in the process. Instead, we manage weeds and use them to our benefit rather than the crop's detriment. Our management plans aren't perfect and we aren't always able to stick to our intended timetable, so we do have to hand weed—but not nearly so much as unprepared planters.

First, we always till fields months before we plant, then let them sit a week or two in warm to hot weather. Next, we irrigate in order to germinate the weed seeds that our cultivation brought to the surface. If weeds come up thinly, we till the field again and plant a green manure crop.

But if weeds come up thickly, we grow the weeds as a green manure. The trick is to turn in the weeds before they go to seed.

Weed management in garlic is especially critical since garlic is often in the ground nine months that span two normal growing seasons. Some weeds germinate best in cool weather, others in hot weather. Garlic gets to enjoy the company of all of them if soil is not properly prepared. Quick green manure crops, such as buckwheat, are an excellent means to allow germination and early growth of weeds that can then be turned into the soil before a new crop of weed seeds is produced.

Growers who plant garlic in wide rows without mulch will need to cultivate regularly in order to control weeds. Best control is achieved by cultivating at a very early stage of weed growth before adequate root systems are formed. If the weeds are allowed to grow more than three inches tall before cultivation, they often re-root and stand back up within a few days, especially if it rains or if nights are dewy. This is especially true of weeds with deep taproots or spreading rhizomatous roots. Garlic is tougher than most vegetables and can withstand some competition, but bulb size may be sacrificed. Even mechanical cultivation usually has to be supplemented by some hand weeding in unprepared soils.

Since we plant intensively in beds we always hand weed, but good advance soil preparation in combination with good mulch usually limits weeding to a single pass in early June. We've seen growers weed constantly from April through July and still harvest a poor crop because weed competition was too great. This is especially predictable on so-called "virgin land" or very old farmland (unused in recent years) because such soils are virtual seedbanks of stored seed just waiting for the soil to be cultivated in order to create the perfect environment for the sudden germination of a ten-year accumulation of weeds and grasses. The resulting vigor and volume can be astounding.

Pre-fertilization

Many garlic farmers fertilize before fall plantings and then again in early spring, especially with a nitrogen source. We haven't found this to be necessary in fertile soils high in organic matter. Garlic is a survivor—it's very adept at finding both moisture and nutrients even when it has to search for them deep in the subsoil. Yet, garlic definitely responds to nitrogen fertilization. Poor to moderately fertile soils will probably grow more vigorous plants and larger bulbs if they are fertilized both fall and spring with nitrogen.

On the other hand, researchers at the University of California found that fertilization of garlic with potassium resulted in no significant increases in yield. Nor were yields significantly improved by addition of zinc or phosphorous sources even when field levels of these nutrients were extremely low. They concluded that zinc, phosphorous and potassium fertilizers should not be applied to garlic crops except in rare cases when soil tests showed extremely low levels.*

I've always assumed that vigorous garlic plants in early spring are not much different than any green leafy vegetable; after all, they're primarily growing green leaves. I expect to see very healthy plants in spring if the soil has between sixty and one hundred pounds of actual nitrogen available per acre. In the poorest soils, I've accomplished this level with a combination of raw organic matter (such as two tons of fresh alfalfa hay per acre about one month prior to planting) and blood meal at a rate of eight hundred pounds per acre. Since the blood meal is twelve to fifteen pounds actual nitrogen per one hundred pounds of meal, eight hundred pounds of blood meal per acre applies 100 to 120 pounds of actual nitrogen per acre. That's enough nitrogen to supply both the decaying alfalfa and the growing garlic the following spring because the blood meal decays and releases its nitrogen slowly over a six to nine week period, depending on soil temperature and moisture, with almost no release at all during cold winter months.

*Tyler, Kent B. et al, "Diagnosing Nutrient Needs of Garlic," *California Agriculture*, 42(2), March-April 1988, p. 28-29.

The application of two tons alfalfa and eight hundred pounds blood meal per acre is an extreme case. In good soil that has been manured sometime during the six months prior to planting garlic, we rarely apply any fall fertilizer. Specific needs will vary depending on specific soils. We've seen generic recommendations for nitrogen applications ranging from a low of thirty-five to sixty pounds of actual nitrogen per acre to a high of two hundred pounds per acre. I recommend something approaching the lower range in most soils. It is worth noting that Egyptian researchers found significant increases in the incidence of storage diseases (such as *Botrytis* and *Penicillium*) in garlic when higher rates of ammonium nitrate fertilizers were used.*

When using organic nitrogen sources such as blood meal, I've seen much better results from incorporation of fertilizer into the soil prior to planting rather than broadcasting or side-dressing the fertilizers after planting. However, I suspect that water-soluble commercial fertilizers would be more appropriately applied as side dressings in moderate amounts of forty to sixty pounds actual nitrogen soon after planting.

Since garlic plants remain in the ground about nine months with active vegetative growth during all but the final month, it's not possible to supply all the nitrogen needs in one application in the fall. We'll discuss spring fertilization in a coming chapter. Just remember garlic stops growing green leaves in late spring and becomes a bulbing plant. High nitrogen levels at that time can delay bulbing and significantly reduce the quality of the harvested bulbs.

Probably the most common mistake that we see new garlic growers make is to assume their unprepared soil is fertile enough for garlic. They don't change their minds until late spring when the garlic plants look small and pale green, often with yellow leaf tips. But it's too late to begin fertilizing after vegetative growth is finished. The lesson is simple. If your soil needs fertilizer, apply it in the fall and again as a side dressing in early spring. Don't wait until May or June.

*Abstract 2422, *Horticultural Abstracts*, 60(4), April 1990, p. 280.

There aren't a lot of widely available organic nitrogen sources outside of dried blood meal (at least in the western U.S.) and moderately fresh manure. But, then, organic farmers with healthy soils rich in humus, good crop rotations, and regular green manure crops don't need large amounts of nitrogen. Whenever possible, I believe nitrogen should come from decaying plant and animal matter to ensure a constant but moderate supply. By contrast, water soluble, commercial fertilizers release large amounts of nitrogen immediately. If the soil is poor in humus, the synthetic nitrogen cannot be stored—it's either used by plants immediately or it's leached out of the soil.

Legumes are ideal as green manure crops because they fix atmospheric nitrogen in the soil and store it for long periods. Clovers and alfalfa serve growers best when allowed to grow for at least one entire season. Quick crops are possible from broad-leaved legumes that prefer warm weather (e.g. beans) or cool weather crops such as field peas and vetch. The green manures are very useful as indicators. Poor growth of the green manure crop indicates poor growth for the cash crops that follow. That's another good reason to start preparing soil at least one year in advance. The green manure crops can point out the specific faults and assets on specific pieces of ground. Successive green manures are like chapters in a story that tell you all about your cropland before you invest in the cash crop. Better to discover an unhappy ending with a stand of buckwheat or clover than with a labor intensive stand of garlic.

Many people assume that garlic needs a soil rich in sulphur because the bulb's taste and medicinal properties are associated with sulphur compounds. Likewise, because garlic is a source of selenium, some growers assume selenium should be applied to the soil. Not so. Selenium is among the many trace elements that occur in relatively small amounts in soils. Many trace elements are necessary to plant growth but also toxic to plants if available in excessive amounts. Garlic concentrates sulphur and selenium in the bulb more than most food plants, but that doesn't mean it needs large amounts per acre in the soil. It does mean that garlic is highly efficient at finding the trace nutrients and accumulating them in the plant. Note, however, that many soils in the western United States **are** actually deficient in selenium. Take a soil test and consult an expert for advice.

Sulphur, on the other hand, is not a trace element. While similar to selenium in its biochemical utilization, sulphur is needed in larger amounts. Some soils are also sulphur deficient, but manure is often a good sulphur source. Again, take a soil test before actually applying sulphur to soils.

I've experimented over the years with the application of various trace elements to garlic ground. I never saw a positive result, but I did see a few adverse reactions. It's quite rare for most soils to be so deficient in trace elements that fertilizer applications are needed. In the rare instances when professional consultants identify such deficiencies, very little actual fertilizer is required to correct them. The addition of a few pounds per acre of some trace elements is enough to cause severe toxic reactions in plants.

There are no panaceas. Good garlic doesn't happen as the result of a recipe of fertilizer (sixty pounds of this and a dash of that). It simply responds to a healthy balance of environmental factors—soil, sun, air, moisture, and nutrients. The key to management is the ability to maintain moderation rather than reacting to extreme deficiencies with excessive solutions.

Summary

The months or years of soil preparation prior to planting are every bit as crucial to garlic production as the nine months that garlic plants are actually in the soil. Site selection is one aspect of preparation. Others are weed control and healthy soil development prior to planting. Good farming requires at least some ability to "look into the future." Green manure crops can serve as windows allowing farmers to see potential problems and head them off. Garlic remains in the soil longer than most common food plants and, therefore, requires more thorough planning and advance preparation.

Selection of Planting Stock

While subspecies *sativum* garlics are generally more vigorous than ophio garlics, there is a direct relationship between the size of the planted clove and the size of the harvested bulb that holds true for all garlic. Surprisingly, there is also a very strong correlation between the size of the seedbulb and the size of the following year's harvested bulb.

Clove and Bulb Size

In our tests with Spanish Roja (subspecies *ophioscorodon*) the weight and size of the seedbulb had a stronger effect on the harvested bulb size than did the weight and size of the planted cloves. Specifically, two seedcloves of identical weight did not tend to produce harvested bulbs with similar weights unless the seedcloves originated from seedbulbs of similar weights. On average, seedbulb size and weight were eight times more significant than seedclove size and weight in determining the size and weight of harvested bulbs. A twelve percent increase in seedbulb size (basically the equivalent of twenty grams or one-quarter inch in bulb diameter) produced significantly larger bulbs at harvest when compared to seedcloves of the same identical weight but from slightly smaller seedbulbs.

Perhaps more significantly, we found that the largest seedbulbs (over two and one half inches in diameter) produced the widest variation in harvested bulbs. Many of the resulting plants had very poor vigor and produced an extreme lack of uniformity in bulb size and quality.

We also found that seedcloves from bulbs with ten or more cloves per bulb consistently had much lower survival rates than other seedcloves. In general, it is the very large bulbs that tend to have the most cloves per bulb (there is a direct correlation between bulb size and number of cloves per bulb), so the largest bulbs would seem to be a poor choice for planting stock.

In short, the size of both the "seedclove" **and** the "seedbulb" is an important consideration when selecting planting stock. We rarely use our largest bulbs as seedbulbs, nor do we use small to medium sized bulbs since their small cloves produce only small to medium sized bulbs. Bulbs two inches to two and one half inches in diameter consistently produce the most desirable results for most northern growers of ophioscorodon garlics.

We haven't tested subspecies *sativum* garlics nearly as thoroughly, but preliminary results suggest that while all the same specific factors apply, the factors are far less critical. Smaller cloves still produce smaller bulbs, but not nearly so much as they do in ophio garlics. The size of the seedbulb is also a factor, but not nearly to the extent that it is in ophio garlics. We still don't use the largest sativum bulbs for planting stock, but it's simply because we don't need to. Large bulbs are worth more money than small and medium size bulbs when sold as tablestock, so why not take the high dollar return and use medium to medium-large bulbs for seed? Variety *sativum* garlics are generally vigorous and productive enough to produce very large bulbs from this somewhat smaller planting stock if they're planted in good soil.

Double Cloves

The occurrence of two bud sprouts inside a single clove skin appears to be largely an ophioscorodon phenomenon that rarely occurs in subspecies *sativum* garlics, at least in northern regions. We performed extensive on-farm research in an effort to determine the cause of double cloves, but the exact "why" and "when" remain somewhat of a mystery. Double cloves are significant because they shorten the storage life of garlic. They also lower the value of planting stock since double cloves produce two or more flat-sided bulbs when they're planted.

It's not always easy to recognize and cull out the doubles during clove popping, yet it's highly desirable to do so if you're producing top-grade market garlic. Restaurants love large double cloves because they peel so easily, but the bulbs need to be used within two or three months of harvest before dehydration and browning of the clove flesh begin.

Double cloves appear malformed, sometimes grotesquely so, as when three or four large cloves are joined together within one continuous clove skin. But subtle doubles (which have nothing to do with the game of tennis) may be very difficult to detect. They often appear as moderately large cloves with a faint depression down the inner or outer side of the clove. The depression may be nearly unrecognizable even when cloves are peeled. Occasionally, they can be recognized by the presence of an odd-shaped true stem on the bottom of the clove(s), or by split clove skins that give the impression of an aborted attempt at clove division.

Some growers think that doubled cloves form very late in the season just before harvest as the result of fertile soil and excessive soil moisture that encourage garlic to keep growing rather than maturing and drying down. The notion is that cloves divide, then grow so much they try to divide again. The notion is simply false.

Clove division in garlic is somewhat of a misnomer. When swelling of the false stem first occurs (about mid May in our region), careful dissection of the swollen area will reveal tiny cloves already formed. The reason is simple. Garlic does not swell into a large solid bulb which then divides into cloves; rather, individual tiny clove buds swell into large cloves that comprise the mature bulb. Formation of clove skins and specialized membranes that surround individual cloves does occur late in the season as part of the maturation process, but actual clove formation takes place very early on. We've detected double cloves just as soon as individual cloves were large enough to recognize. This suggests to us that both the number of cloves per bulb and the occurrence of double cloves are probably already determined before bulbing begins.

We also know that the total number of leaves per plant

is largely determined very early in the fall. Dissection of cloves with short two to three inch sprouts reveals all the plant leaves already formed inside the clove, folded tightly inside one another at the base of the sprout. The leaves elongate one at a time as the season progresses. Each leaf has clove buds in the axil where the leaf joins the true stem, but only the last two leaves (the innermost leaves) eventually swell those buds into cloves in ophio garlics. The number of fertile buds per leaf can range from approximately one to ten, but in ophio garlics it is more commonly three to five per leaf.

When bulbing (bud swelling) begins in late spring it is because of hormonal activity that stimulates the growth of specialized leaves known as "storage leaves," or, more commonly, as cloves. The general process of bulbing is initiated by a combination of factors that are not fully understood. Increased day length is definitely a strong factor, but so are temperature, soil fertility, and plant vigor. Even the storage temperatures experienced before planting have a marked effect on the time of bulbing and subsequent plant maturation.

Our best guess is that too much or too little of a specific hormone associated with the swelling of the storage leaf causes some buds to receive a garbled message resulting in double cloves. There may even be a direct relationship between the size of the bud and the probability of double cloves; that is, large sized buds may tend to produce double sprouts. Or, buds positioned too close together may end up inside a single storage leaf.

Whatever the specific cause of double cloves, our research shows there is absolutely no genetic inheritance involved in the occurrence of double cloves. Some growers discard all seedbulbs that have double cloves, but we've determined there is absolutely no relationship between the incidence of double cloves in the parent bulb and the resulting generation of bulbs. The causes are environmental.

On the other hand, there is a distinct genetic difference between strains. Some ophio garlics simply have a high predisposition to produce double cloves under certain environmental conditions while others very rarely produce them under any conditions. Each strain of garlic has a fairly constant percentage of cloves likely to contain multiple embryos. The percentage varies slightly year to year based on variations in soil and climate, but does not vary genetically from bulb to bulb; rather, double cloves are the random expressions of a predetermined genetic probability. The result is that the incidence of double cloves varies annually, and large bulbs (with many cloves) are always more likely to have double cloves than are small bulbs (with few cloves).

The environmental factors affecting the incidence of double cloves seem to include a few that can be managed by the grower. Highly fertile soil tends to produce very large bulbs with many cloves so that every bulb may have at least one double clove. Moderation in application of fertilizers will reduce plant vigor, bulb size, and the number of bulbs with double cloves.

Another factor is the time of planting (which will be discussed momentarily).

Softneck garlics very rarely produce double cloves in northern climates. (We're not sure about southern climates, though L.K. Mann mentions them in his studies of California Late and California Early—both subspecies *sativum*—as grown in central California.) In a few Artichoke cultigens, and especially in some of the Silverskin garlics, there is a strong tendency in our region for large outer cloves to be subdivided into two or more smaller cloves when soils are fertile and conditions are conducive to very large bulb size. But each of the smaller cloves is cleanly formed with its own clove skin and a single sprout. Thus, the occurrence of flat-sided bulbs resulting from a single planted clove with two sprouts is extremely low for sativum garlics in northern regions.

I suspect that softneck garlics, whose primary reproductive tendency is clove formation rather than bulbil production, simply do a better job of producing cloves. The exact factors controlling bolting (flower stalk and bulbil production) are not clearly understood, but early maturity and rapid initiation of bulbing both seem to deter bolting. Softneck garlics do grow more rapidly than ophio garlics (despite generally slower breaking of dormancy and initiation of sprouting) and mature earlier as well. Ophioscorodon garlics produce large bulbs and cloves basically as the result of damage to or removal of the flower stalk and its umbel (containing the bulbils). The capacity of ophio garlics to produce cloves has undoubtedly increased over the millennia as the result of human selection and evolution, but one could almost state that clove production in ophio garlics is a secondary (or backup) ability that does not significantly manifest itself until the primary reproductive habit is prevented and/or the plant is placed in a highly fertile, pampered environment unlike the harsh environment its ancestors originated in.

The increased occurrence of double cloves in very large-bulbed ophio garlics is only one of several factors affecting overall bulb quality. It is ironic that consumers generally prefer large bulbs when there can be little doubt that overall quality of ophio garlics deteriorates as bulb size increases. Garlic growers must constantly be in search of the "happy medium," that optimal range where size is large, but not so large that quality is seriously affected. To find the optimum range, additional factors besides the size of seedcloves and seedbulbs must be considered.

Time of Planting

Most northern growers plant garlic in October. A few at high elevations or in early winter regions plant in late September. The specific week of the year that cloves are planted can significantly affect both the quality of the harvested crop and the time of maturity.

Garlic planted too late in the fall will not begin good root growth until the following spring. Since root growth always precedes sprouting and leaf growth, late planted garlic gets off to a slow start in the spring. The decreased number of growing days before the summer solstice means smaller plants and correspondingly smaller bulb size.

Garlic can also be planted too early. The obvious reason is too much top growth before winter can sometimes result in winter damage. We haven't found this to be a serious problem in test plantings as early as late August. While some leaves do die back, winter-kill seems to occur only when both the clove and roots are suddenly frozen—not the leaves.

However, there are more subtle reasons not to plant too early, particularly for ophio garlics. Ophios have an odd quirk about them in that storage temperatures prior to planting can affect the character of harvested bulbs every bit as much as the actual growing conditions *after* the garlic is planted. The same factors affect subspecies *sativum*, but not as strongly.

One of the keys is high storage temperatures. When ophio garlics are planted in late August or early September in our climate, they rarely experience temperatures below fifty degrees Fahrenheit in storage. I can't tell you the specific reasons, but such ophio garlic tends to produce significantly more cloves per bulb (thus, cloves are smallish), and far more double cloves per bulb. Our late summer plantings (late August to early September) of ophio garlics usually produce inferior quality bulbs despite large bulb size. Cloves are flat, tall, and wedge-shaped rather than plump and round. Clove skins are a very light tan color rather than reddish-brown. Bulbs are noticeably lighter in weight than those from October and November plantings, and they dehydrate rapidly in storage. This suggests lower soluble solids and a higher water content. The higher incidence of double cloves with split or broken clove skins accentuates the problem of rapid dehydration in storage.

Late fall plantings have the opposite effect on ophio garlics. Bulbs have fewer cloves per bulb (often only four to six) and very strong character and color. The plump, round cloves are very dense with tight clove skins and they can usually be easily counted without even removing the bulb wrappers. Clove skins are a dark reddish-brown. Bulbs are dense and heavy, indicating they are high in soluble solids, and they store much longer than bulbs from October plantings. Double cloves are very rare in late October and November plantings.

Our findings for northern grown ophio garlics basically correspond to the findings of L.K. Mann and his colleagues when they tested sativum garlics in central California. In addition, Mann found that prolonged cold storage at temperatures close to freezing or above seventy degrees Fahrenheit (prior to planting) often produced rough bulbs with poor character, sometimes even producing secondary leaf growth and multi-stemmed plants. Pre-planting storage temperatures also had marked effects on the subsequent initiation of root growth and sprouting. Earliest root growth and sprouting occurred when bulbs were stored at temperatures of about forty to fifty degrees Fahrenheit for several weeks prior to planting. Those stored at about forty-three degrees often produced the earliest roots and sprouts, but those stored at fifty degrees often produced more vigorous root and top growth after sprouting and emergence. By contrast, bulbs stored at lower temperatures emerged later and grew most rapidly, but also matured earliest and produced the least uniformity and character. Bulbs stored at high temperatures before planting sometimes failed to bulb at all.

The occurrence of double cloves, then, is directly related to time of planting, and it's only one aspect of a more general quality described as "bulb roughness." We know there is a direct relationship between soil fertility, plant vigor, and bulb size. We also know very large bulbs have both more cloves per bulb and more double cloves than do small bulbs. The relationship between size and vigor on the one hand, and double cloves, secondary leaf growth, and generally rough bulbs on the other, is unmistakable. It makes good sense that late summer plantings in August or September produce larger bulbs than fall plantings because of the increased number of growing days prior to initiation of bud swelling and bulbing. Throw in the effect of either no cold or too much cold temperature prior to planting and you have the phenomenon know as "rough bulbs."

As a result, some growers may wish to pre-condition garlic prior to planting, especially if they live in southern climates. Garlic root growth occurs primarily in response to humidity and is largely independent of sprouting. The critical humidity is somewhere around 65% to 70%. Most soils with moderate moisture levels will induce root growth within one to two weeks after planting, so no pre-conditioning should be necessary. But sprouting occurs independently of root growth and primarily as the result of temperature. Growers who want to encourage rapid emergence after planting may wish to purposely subject seedbulbs to temperatures between approximately forty-three to fifty degrees Fahrenheit for two weeks or more prior to planting of cloves. Most growers do not feel pre-conditioning gains any significant advantage. We concentrate on good root growth before winter and let the garlic decide for itself when to sprout and emerge from the soil.

Fall Journal Entries

September 22—We finished cleaning the Spanish Roja (subspecies *ophioscorodon*) from the Highway Tract today. Return on pounds planted for all the other ophio garlics from that tract was 9.7 to 1, which is very respectable, but the Roja was only 5.8 to 1. It didn't appreciate the mild winter and wet spring. The Roja yield was our third lowest in fourteen years.

The total volume of garlic this year was our largest ever, but the overall return on pounds planted was quite disappointing. It was far lower than expected and lower than our long term average. The reason is no mystery.

We planted garlic in two separate fields last fall, one of them our own ground and one a small leased parcel directly east of our orchard. The lease land was not in great shape—we knew that. We actually felt forced to lease it because we couldn't afford to have an abandoned orchard adjacent to our own organic orchard. The trees had been felled and left in the field next to their sprouting stumps one and one half years before we took possession in July. It was quite a task to remove the stumps and till the ground repeatedly in hot weather in an effort to kill out the witch grass, orchard grass, morning glory, and other undesirable odds and ends.

By mid-September it looked as if we'd been successful, so much so that we decided to plant half our garlic there. In retrospect it was an incredibly stupid decision—the kind experienced farmers aren't supposed to make, but often do when the current circumstances and the heat of the moment cloud their better judgement and tempt them to act like fools. The land we had originally slated for garlic was not quite as ready as I would have liked. Our annual increases in garlic production had crept up on us and shortened our normal three year rotation to two years. When the lease land was all tilled, I made the sudden decision to plant it to garlic so I could save part of our own land for that third year of normal rotation.

The rest of our reasoning seemed quite logical. Garlic demand had been consistently high. We'd never been able to fill all the orders. The lease land might not produce the best garlic in the world, but it should produce decent bulbs while allowing us to "kill two birds with one stone." We should be able to again increase overall production while saving our better land for one more year of green manuring. What actually happened is already history. Garlic yields on our own land were very good—with the exception of our main crop, Spanish Roja—but those on the lease land were the worst we'd ever experienced. After fourteen years of preaching that new garlic growers shouldn't jump into production on new ground, I obviously should have known better. I did know better. I got exactly what I had predicted all those other eager growers would get—major disappointment.

Ironically, the lease land garlic is storing better than the bulbs grown in our best soil, even when compared to small bulbs of similar size. The lower tilth and lower fertility of the old orchard ground resulted in small (very small) compact bulbs that were very dense and solid. They probably had a lot more taste and quality concentrated in them than the large "Premium" sized whoppers from the Highway Tract. Bulb and clove colors were also impressive. I've always suspected that ophio garlics gain lots of bulb size only as they lose quality. Looks are often deceiving. Too bad the yield was so low in actual pounds that we lost money.

October 1—We're ready to plant the new crop in about two weeks. The planting stock consists of very firm 2" to 2.5" bulbs from the Highway Tract "Q" series, which we've been selecting as planting stock for six years. Most of the other planting quality ophio bulbs have already been shipped to other growers across the nation. The biggest bulbs, the soft bulbs, and the smallest bulbs go to California, but most of it won't get shipped until later this month. We still have several thousand pounds of table stock stored in the warehouse. That's more than normal for this time of year, but then we grew more garlic this year.

It's been a very warm fall so far. Temperatures were in the nineties all through the third week of September and in the eighties this past week. The warehouse temperature hasn't fallen below fifty degrees Fahrenheit (obviously) and I probably won't have to build any fires in the old woodstove until November, not unless a rainy spell raises the humidity above 70%. Partial dehydration and initial softening of some of the largest ophio bulbs are the only early reminders so far that ophio garlics want to grow in the fall and won't store forever. There are no signs yet of swollen root nodules at the base of the cloves. When they start appearing, I know it's time to get the remaining ophio stock shipped out as soon as possible. Sprouting is largely independent of root swell, but it often follows within two to four weeks.

Garlic has been out of the ground exactly three months now and it's already time to plant. These bulbs just don't like to be out of the soil for very long. Not that the Artichoke garlics aren't storing well. They'll still be firm and fit three months from now. But we don't have the option to plant in three months this far north.

Harvest was early this year, June 26th to July 4th; in fact, the earliest ever. When the absolutely abnormal (in fact, inexcusable) thirty-five days of rain finally stopped in mid-June, I was afraid to irrigate again. Of course, it turned very hot very suddenly and dry down occurred very rapidly toward the end of June. If I had irrigated one more time in mid-June.... Seems like I say that every year. Anyway, we'll find out within the next thirty to sixty days whether this is an average or a good storage year for ophio garlics. In a bad year we'd already be finding serious bulb softening and swollen roots by now. If it's an average year the bulbs will be okay at least until

Thanksgiving. If it's a good year they can sit until Christmas.

October 7—The garlic fields are ready for planting. The final buckwheat crop was turned under September 16. One week later we spread four hundred pounds per acre of blood meal and tilled again. That left one more week to complete a final irrigation before the Reclamation District shut down the system. We got it all watered. Soils seemed a bit on the damp side one week ago, but they're just right now. In fact, if it doesn't rain, we'll probably finish planting the far end of the field in the dust. Moisture shouldn't be a problem this year. It still seems unseasonably warm, but next week we'll probably put off planting until almost noon each day when the frost is gone and our fingers can handle the cloves with some nimbleness. At least that's what's been typical in past years. (This year hasn't been very typical!)

In their current condition, the garlic fields look barren. It's not often they lie this naked and unprotected. The field where garlic was harvested in July had one buckwheat crop and is now a thick, verdant carpet of rye grain and red clover. It's planted so thickly it will take a little work to turn it into the soil next April in preparation for my wife's garden. Even the current years garden (which will be garlic next fall) is sporting an explosion of green leaf tips (rye) and fuzzy vetch sprouts despite the fact we were harvesting food from it only ten days ago. Of course, the fall plantings of carrots and broccoli are still fresh-looking at the far edge where they are silhouetted against the garlic field. The garlic field...what passerby would suspect that bare soil to be only one week from planting?

I love this time of year. Most folks are winding down and preparing for a long winter. The growing season is over for them. I'm told late fall and early winter can even be very depressing to some people—such as farmers who've just finished a bad year (Ha, Ha!). Not so at Filaree Farm. Even if the apples lose money (like they have these past three years), we don't have time to brood. October is garlic planting month, and I look at it literally as the beginning of a new growing season right on the heels of our other harvests. Actually, the Granny Smith, Winesap, and Fuji apples haven't even been picked yet. We'll plant garlic, then harvest the late winter apples and spend the rest of the year packing and shipping both garlic and fruit. January through March is pruning time in the orchard, and the garlic usually emerges and greens the fields before the pruning is finished. It pops up before the lilacs or the pussy willows bloom, before the dormant fruit buds begin to swell, and even before the first meal of fresh green nettles.

In many ways, garlic weaves our year into one long uninterrupted orgy of growth and harvest. There really isn't a break anywhere. Most farmers' years are composed of start, run, stop, and rest (known as spring, summer, fall, and winter to non-farmers). But we've grown accustomed to steady, year round growth and activity at Filaree. Our lives and our farm would actually seem empty without garlic in the ground nine months, and in the warehouse the other three. The stage of the garlic is how we gauge the month of the year and the particular season. And it's almost planting time.

I'd better be going out to the garlic field to mark some beds.

Summary

Regarding planting dates, the "happy medium" that most growers seek translates into the month of October. That's the intermediate period of approximately four weeks that results in optimal quality, character, **and** productivity in most years. The optimal window may encompass the last half of September in the far north or at high altitudes where winter arrives early. It may also stretch into November in a few regions. In California and the deep south, it may even stretch into December.

All the aforementioned factors help to explain why so many ophio garlics tend to perform poorly in southern regions that reach from central California to Florida— wherever winters are so mild that vegetative growth proceeds all winter. Softneck garlics are better adapted to long seasons, mild winters, and fertile environments because they're more highly domesticated. Ophio garlics perform best where winters are long and the season of vegetative growth is relatively short.

Medium large bulbs usually make the best seed bulbs for both ophio and sativum garlics, but somewhat smaller cloves of sativum may be planted while still producing very large bulbs in good environments. Sativums have a longer period of dormancy and take longer to germinate than ophio garlics, but they grow faster and mature faster than ophio garlics. Some moderation in soil fertility and size of the planting stock generally yields the most desirable results.

Fall Chores

The breaking of seedbulbs into individual cloves is called "clove popping." It is one of the most tedious tasks involved in garlic production and generally takes two to three times longer than the actual planting of the cloves. Yet, clove poppers must also make some of the most critical decisions determining the quality of the eventual harvest.

Clove Popping

Only the firmest bulbs should be selected for planting stock. A clove popper's first duty is to squeeze the bulb gently to test for softness. Soft bulbs indicate dehydration and less vigorous cloves, not to mention the increased possibility of molds. A rock hard condition is best. A "little give" is okay. Soft bulbs are better off discarded. We save the soft bulbs for processing.

It's best not to pop bulbs apart into individual cloves more than a few days prior to actual planting. Separation of cloves from the mother bulb seems to encourage swelling of root nodules and the initiation of sprout growth at somewhat lower humidities and higher temperatures than for whole bulbs. This activity is signalled by an increased emission of carbon dioxide. The increased exchange of gases through the clove skin signals that cloves are no longer in a deep state of rest, so it is desirable to plant them as soon as possible. As usual, the tendency is far more pronounced in ophio garlics than in sativums.

The popping process often breaks clove skins, especially on ophio garlics, sometimes exposing entire cloves. These so-called "naked" cloves are fine to plant as long as the flesh itself is not bruised or broken (as with a fingernail), but they can't be left sitting around one or two weeks or they will dehydrate.

There is an art to popping bulbs into cloves because firm bulbs don't want to break apart. I start by running my thumbnail around the woody stem just above the cloves. This breaks the bulb wrappers. Next, grab the stem as close to the top of the bulb as possible and twist one vigorous turn. An experienced popper can accomplish both these maneuvers in one single motion. Believe me, good poppers are a blessing.

Once the bulb wrappers are broken and loosened at the top of the bulb, they sluff off the rest of the bulb with only slight pressure from a slightly moistened thumb. Too much moisture makes the wrappers stick to your thumb. The pressure must be applied in a "down and out" motion as if trying to get your thumb underneath the wrappers. Simple downward pressure either *against* the bulb surface or *along* the surface will only wear out a good thumb.

It's not always necessary to remove all the bulb wrappers. Ophio garlics are divided into two unequal halves by a single bulb wrapper. Almost as soon as you can see the division point, you can usually break the bulb into its two natural halves. Further division of the cloves is then a simple task. Don't try to divide the bulb in half just anyplace—you'll probably end up with very sore hands and a lot of bruised garlic cloves.

Softneck garlics pop apart similarly, but it's often necessary to break the bulb wrapper at the top of the bulb for each successive clove layer rather than just once at the outset. Softneck garlics take longer to pop apart because bulb wrappers are tighter and there are more total clove layers (and more total cloves).

Inexperienced growers make common mistakes while popping apart their planting stock. They tend to **throw** all the cloves carelessly into a bag or box without realizing that garlic bruises. Every bruise is an easy target for fungi and disease organisms in the soil. Bruises also allow more rapid dehydration. Even minor bruises may potentially weaken a plant by robbing the clove of some of the early moisture and nutrients it must supply to the young sprout until both roots and leaves are developed.

Secondly, inexperienced growers may break the clove stem at the clove base. Garlic bulbs in less than firm, hard condition have a tendency to suffer broken plates on individual cloves. The basal plate (the hard dark scab at the bottom of the clove) is actually the true stem of the future garlic plant. When a portion of the true stem breaks off as the clove is separated from the mother bulb, the garlic literally has a broken stem. Root buds occur around the outer edge of the true stem, especially on the side farthest from the center of the old bulb, so a broken stem means that root buds have been lost—a less vigorous plant is the result. Serious damage to the true stem can lead to clove rot.

In short, poppers need to quickly examine the bottom of each clove and discard those with damaged stems. Slight damage may not pose a problem, but the key is to use firm, hard bulbs whose cloves separate cleanly without any damage to the true stem. (We toss damaged cloves into a cull food box and sell them at a reduced rate to salsa makers or other food processors who will use them quickly.)

Poppers also need to decide which cloves are too small for planting. There is a direct relationship between the size of the planted clove and the size of the harvested bulb when all other factors are equal. You might try weighing a clove on a postal scale every now and then. We seldom plant cloves smaller than five grams in weight if we're trying to grow large-bulbed market garlic. Six to nine gram cloves are probably ideal for ophio garlics, and the range is wider for softneck garlics which grow more vigorously. We plant the largest cloves as well, but they tend to be more variable in vigor than medium to large sized cloves.

Once general guidelines for clove size have been established, lay a few sample cloves in plain sight for quick comparisons. You'll find many cloves that seem borderline in size, and there are two ways to deal with them. One is to make a hard and fast rule, such as "When in doubt, cast them out." That way the poppers can make a quick decision without wasting time studying the clove.

Another method is to glance quickly at the true stem on

the bottom of the clove. The size of the true stem corre-
lates directly to the size and number of root buds on the
clove. Cloves that are borderline in size in addition to having small true stems are guaranteed to produce small
plants and small bulbs.

There is an old and persistent myth that the small inner
cloves of softneck garlics should not be planted because
they will not grow. It's just not true. If they're too small
then they'll produce only small bulbs, but all the cloves
(and bulbils) will sprout and grow if given the chance.
The shape of the clove has absolutely nothing to do with
the shape of the bulb that will be produced. Very odd-
shaped cloves produce very normal bulbs. Gardeners
who don't care about uniformly large bulb size can replant
practically all the cloves in the bulb. Commercial growers
will probably cast aside the smaller cloves.

Finally, poppers need to constantly be on the lookout
for damaged or diseased bulbs and cloves. For example,
if a bulb has one obviously rotten clove before the bulb
wrappers are even removed, my advice is "throw it out."
Don't try to save the good cloves. The chances of breaking open that bulb and spreading the spores of a fungus
over an entire batch of good cloves is simply too great.
In fact, that's the most common way of spreading blue-
green penicillium molds. When poppers find mold, they
should stop immediately and dispose of the bulb very
carefully. They should not throw the bulb across the
room and should not pass it around the table for everyone else to see and handle, thus, contaminating their
hands and clothes.

The general rule is to plant only the best cloves from
the best bulbs. Avoid damage or disease of any kind because if you don't discard it prior to planting, you're liable
to end up having to discard a lot more plants later on
when it spreads through the planted field. Even bruised
cloves and bulbs should be avoided—bruises don't
spread disease, but they provide a suitable site for fungi
and diseases which then spread themselves.

Popped cloves can be stored a day or two in netted
bags, boxes, or grocery bags. If unforeseen circumstances force you to store popped cloves more than two days

before planting, make sure the cloves have good air circulation. Don't pack forty pounds of cloves into any container for very long because they will sweat, then heat up, and mold. Keep popped cloves out of direct sunlight and away from heat. Store them below room temperature if possible.

Incidentally, clove poppers should always be on the lookout for mutations that display different traits than the normal bulbs. These usually occur as single bulb mutations which get thrown in the cull box because they "look weird" compared to the rest of the bulbs. Some very unique and productive garlic strains have been discovered as single bulb mutations, but a lot more have probably been lost to the world because they appeared abnormal.

Clove Planting

First and foremost, make sure your planters understand which end of the clove goes down! It seems inconceivable, but I've seen whole beds planted upside down. The garlic that managed to figure out which way was really up before it ran out of stored food was not very vigorous, and the twisted necks usually deformed the bulb. Process garlic can perhaps be planted in any position, but not gourmet market garlic.

It's unwise to assume that your hired help knows all the basics. Better to simply show them a clove and point out that the scab end (or basal plate) goes down. That's the true stem from which the roots will grows. Garlic cloves are not seeds—they're plants. They don't like to be planted upside down any more than a tomato transplant or an apple tree.

Second, beds and rows should be marked in advance of planting. The clove spacing should also be marked in the soil or else planters must carry a measuring device such as a planting stick with marks at appropriate intervals. If very much acreage is being planted, I highly recommend a device with wheels. My wife made a five-row bed marker from an old wooden spool in about an hour. It marked entire beds into five inch by eight inch squares in a matter of minutes.

Actual plant spacing is probably one of the hardest choices most growers will face. Almost no two growers plant at the same spacing. I've wondered if a grower's plant spacing wasn't like a fingerprint that distinguished him/her from all others.

The first choice is between rows and beds. If you choose rows, then the distance between rows should be determined by the specific tools or machines you use to cultivate the middles between the rows. The same may be true of the distance between beds. We've seen row spacings up to thirty-six inches in poor soil.

The sage old planter will tell you the tendency is to plant too close—as if the little cloves were never going to grow up to be two to three foot tall plants with spreading leaves and roots. That's an especially bad error when manual laborers will be expected to hand weed while maneuvering on their hands and knees. More experienced farmers don't spend long hours on hands and knees, nor do they expect manual laborers to perform the chore for them. Instead, they use tools (remember those labor saving devices) such as hula or onion hoes. Whatever your method, space the garlic plants to accommodate it.

In terms of bulb size, most growers would like to produce two inch to two and one half inch diameter bulbs (if not bigger). To reach two and one half inches in diameter cloves will need to be spaced an absolute minimum two and one half inches apart (that is, mature bulbs would be touching each other), but most growers allow more room than this. Row plantings are more closely spaced than beds. I've seen fresh market garlic planted as close as every three inches, but I think a very fertile soil is required. A basic rule of thumb is a distance twice the desired bulb diameter. Therefore, bed spacings of five inches by eight inches are fairly common for ophio garlics, and perhaps six inches by eight inches for Artichoke garlics. Four to six inch spacing is more common for row plantings.

Bed width is also important because plants in the middle of the bed must compete harder for sunlight when beds are too wide. These plants tend to grow taller with longer, narrower leaves whenever beds are more than five plants wide unless the space between plants is more that eight inches. Hand weeders can't easily reach across or through beds that are four feet wide. Therefore, beds are commonly three to five plants wide and fifteen to thirty inches wide.

The width of the work aisle *between the beds* is often viewed as incidental—until someone has to actually perform work in them. If aisles are too narrow, laborers don't have room to perform even simple physical tasks. The result is usually neglected garlic overrun with rank weed growth because hand weeders can't physically operate in the small space provided them. Beginning garlic growers often forget needed work space and tend to cram plants together in order to get high production per acre—a notion that has something to do with efficiency and economics. The problem with economic equations is they usually leave out people and plants.

Most years our aisles are the same width as our beds (i.e. fifty percent of the ground is actually planted). That may sound inefficient but our yield is four to five tons per acre. We tried narrower aisles and were unhappy with the cramped work space. California growers get higher yields, but they're often growing softneck varieties for processing while using high fertilizer and herbicide inputs.

Depth of planting is an important consideration. I like about one inch of topsoil on top of the clove before the beds are mulched. Many northern growers seem to prefer two to three inches of cover, especially if they don't mulch. The extra few inches of soil helps prevent cloves from being heaved out of the ground as the soil surface repeatedly freezes and thaws in fall and spring.

Deep clove planting may also protect the cloves from freezing too suddenly, but in poorer soils I think it also makes it harder for the garlic to size up when it's bulbing. The deeper the planting and the poorer the soil, the less air and nutrients that will be readily available to the shallow roots. We've heard of growers placing cloves a full six inches beneath the surface, but we can't recommend more than three or four inches of depth. Deeper plantings often lead to slower and more variable germination, smaller (although perhaps hardier and sturdier) plants, and generally smaller bulbs at harvest. Deep planted garlic is certainly harder to pull or dig from the soil at harvest, and it may tend to have thinner more brittle bulb wrappers that are easily lost during curing and cleaning. None of these factors necessarily results in lower quality garlic—in fact, bulbs may store better—but the garlic is generally harder to manage and harder to size up. We hope to do more specific research on the effects of depth of planting (research idea number 168).

The only good reason we can think of to plant cloves six inches deep is if you're a dryland farmer in a semi-arid region, but I suspect, even then, a catch basin or "sunken bed" may be a better alternative. By planting in a cavity or depression, rainwater is caught and concentrated in planted areas and moisture from evaporation loss is minimized because the soil surface is protected from the drying effects of searing winds. Basin planting is a long proven technique of native Americans in the southwest. It should probably be employed far more than it actually is in the western United States.

We like to pat down the earth after planting each row of cloves. Firmed earth insures good contact between clove and soil particles. Air pockets around the cloves could be conducive to both fungal growth and clove dehydration.

Next, you need to consider irrigation. Many growers in the western United States like to irrigate shortly after planting. Others, like me, would like to irrigate but can't because they live within a Federal Reclamation District that shuts off all irrigation water by about the first of October. October heat-spells and Indian Summers are not uncommon in our region. Some years the garlic fields are dusty before we finish planting. In those years, we mulch as soon as possible and then hope for fall rains that sometimes never materialize at all. Somehow, the garlic always manages to flourish.

It is best to take the planted crop into winter with some moisture in the soil, but wet soils should be avoided as they freeze quickly and deeply when the mercury plunges below zero and stays there a week or two. When you can form a handful of soil into a ball in your hand without squeezing any water out and without the surface of the ball feeling sticky or wet, then you have plenty of soil moisture.

Mulching

I remember lots of frustrations with mulches as a young, inexperienced gardener. Tree leaves and, in some cases, pine needles were always the easiest materials to collect and spread, so we used them without much forethought. The results were rarely satisfactory. Either the weeds grew robustly as if they preferred the mulched environment, or nothing grew at all, including our crops. In the latter case, we assumed that the mulch was too thick, but too toxic may have been closer to the truth.

Today I am older, wiser, and more patient—not a saint, mind you, but I mulch with the dedication of a champion chess player and the fervent sincerity of a young priest. One of the lessons I've learned with age and experience is that the activities and relationships on or very near the soil surface are often far more important than those occurring three to eight inches beneath the surface. That makes the specific kind of mulch, the depth of the mulch, and the time of application all very critical.

The advantages of mulches are well understood if not always fully realized, but the potential disadvantages and disasters are far less understood by gardeners and farmers. The trick is to make management decisions that avoid disasters and maximize benefits.

Let's quickly review the potential benefits of mulch so we can clearly understand our intended purpose.

Mulch moderates soil conditions. Like a good referee, a good mulch will prevent outrageous excesses in temperature and moisture levels so plants can enjoy a "level playing field" with well established rules and boundaries. Bare soil can reach temperatures of 120 degrees Fahrenheit beneath a hot summer sun. During spring and fall the same bare soil can fluctuate more than fifty degrees Fahrenheit in less than twelve hours as the surface cooks in afternoon sun, then rapidly cools and freezes at night. The physical movement of soil particles under such ex-

treme fluctuations can be enormous. Soil/plant relationships can literally be ripped apart as the topsoil expands
and contracts, first heaving, then settling. Some plants
can't survive the shock of such treatment at all. Most
plants survive but are unable to concentrate on the serious business of rapid, vigorous growth.

In contrast, properly mulched soil surfaces maintain relatively constant temperatures with very little physical
movement to interrupt the capillary movement of the soil
solution and nutrients. Plant growth may slow dramatically
on cold nights and increase rapidly on warm days, but
the well-moderated temperature fluctuations don't occur as
sudden and shocking physical interruptions.

Good mulches also moderate soil moisture levels, primarily by preventing rapid midday evaporation. Soil surfaces are not exposed to the hot sun or to drying winds,
so they retain moisture longer. Plants can benefit enor-
mously from the maintenance of more constant and more
nearly optimal moisture levels. In combination with moderated soil temperatures, nutrient availability remains more
constant.

Without mulch, rapid changes in soil moisture and temperature cause extreme changes in soil chemical reactions.
As soil changes from hot to cold and wet to dry, corresponding changes occur in soil pH as nutrients are first
tied up and inactive, then chemically active and potentially
excessively available a few hours later. The constant and
extreme daily changes in the fundamental chemistry of un-
mulched soil pose a myriad of actual chemical hazards for
actively growing plants.

Good mulches also moderate the effects of excessive
rainfall by soaking up moisture and preventing erosion
due to water runoff. Heavy rains don't fall directly on the
soil surface where each droplet is a potential bomb that
can explode on impact and destroy the structure of the
topsoil by blasting soil particles apart. The undesirable result is a layer of tiny fragmented soil particles that bake as
they dry to form a nearly impenetrable surface blocking
the movement of water and the exchange of gases such
as oxygen, nitrogen, and carbon dioxide.

Good mulches protect soils from extreme physical,

chemical, and biological variations that may hinder or actually harm plants.

So, what are the potential disadvantages of these miracle materials known as mulches? Heavy mulches may prevent cold soils from warming up in spring. They may even prevent hot soils from cooling off if they hold in too much heat. They may also keep wet soils from drying out, or they may hold so much moisture that none reaches the soil beneath the mulch. In short, good mulch has to breath. But, if the mulch is too porous and loose, then the exchange of heat and moisture between the soil and air will not be moderated; if the mulch is too solid and tight, then no exchange occurs at all.

The structure of the mulch is especially critical regarding the interchange of moisture, particularly the penetration of moisture into the soil. Coarse, unchopped straw with long, dry stems stacks loosely and doesn't settle well, so it poses no problem where water is concerned. Fine sawdust or thick, wet, unchopped leaves may form impenetrable barriers. Water moves through soil by capillary action involving soil particles and the empty space between particles. Extreme changes in particle size or shape can destroy capillary action just like a solid barrier. A layer of manure or sawdust on top of the soil can actually prevent filtration of water into the soil. For example, I saw young fruit trees die from lack of water despite an obviously muddy solution of wet manure piled around the tree trunks, and the grower thought the trees had been "burned" from excessive nitrogen and nutrients in the manure. But, when I dug a hole near the tree, I found bone dry earth just under the wet manure.

The lesson is that mulches should be moderate in texture and depth if they are expected to moderate the soil environment. I avoid light, coarse materials, and I avoid thick, heavy materials. I use chopped straw rather than whole straw. If I intend to use manures, I age or compost it, and I shred leaves or make sure they are partially decayed.

Some mulching materials contain toxic components potentially harmful to plants. Raw manures and sawdust are probably the worst offenders, but fresh tree leaves (such as oak) and sewage sludge are just as suspect. For example, sawdust contains varying amounts of turpins, resins, and pitches, depending on its age and the kind of trees it came from. These materials may be leached into soil by rainwater if they're water soluble, or released as the sawdust decays. In the soil these compounds often act like herbicides by inhibiting plant growth or even killing plants. When sawdust is used as a mulch, it's perhaps not as potentially harmful as sawdust that's turned into the soil. Theoretically, the mulch is a buffer. It's not supposed to rapidly decay and release chemical compounds; in fact, sawdust can only decay very slowly because it's high in cellulose and carbon which require enormous amounts of nitrogen. But, the potential for damage is always present.

Growers should consider not only the physical texture of potential mulch materials, but also its chemical content, its probable rate of decay, its moisture holding capacity, and possible contamination from chemical toxins, pesticide residues, or noxious weed seeds. The latter is a particularly bad problem in the western United States where any application of old straw or tree leaves may turn out to be a quick way to seed your fields to Diffuse Knapweed, Canada Thistle, Morning Glory, or dozens of other very noxious plants.

Garlic growers do have an easier time than some growers simply because garlic is a basically tough plant. The first leaf is a very specialized structure (not a true leaf) whose only purpose is to push up through the soil (and any other barriers) and find sunlight. Its tough tip can force its way through tight soils and thick mulches that many weeds cannot negotiate. The specialized leaf can't grow very tall, however, before ordinary plant leaves take over. If mulches are too deep, the normal leaves won't be able to push through.

My favorite mulch is fresh grass clippings from my orchard. I simply stop mowing the orchard in late August so the grass is thick and tall by late October. We mow the orchard one last time after planting the garlic, rake it by hand, and mulch the garlic field as soon after planting as possible. The fresh grass is much easier to handle than dried straw. It's still green, so it actually releases some nitrogen in the fall as it dries and begins to decay. Some is in the form of ammonia that's lost into the air, but some is also carried into the topsoil by rainwater.

The fresh grass is applied evenly in a fluffy layer about six inches deep. That allows some transfer of air, water, and heat after it's applied. Even in the spring after winter snows have matted the grass into a thin layer only one inch or less in thickness, the grass breathes. It also blocks direct sunlight from heating the soil surface and that prevents a lot of weed seed germination until late spring when the grass mulch finally begins to seriously decay in the heat of late May. By then the garlic is finished with vigorous leaf growth—it can handle a little competition from weeds.

The gradually decaying grass mulch also allows the soil surface to begin drying in June and July. That's ideal for garlic which changes from a vigorous leafy plant in early spring to a bulbing plant in late spring. The rate of disintegration of the grass mulch happens to coincide almost perfectly with the needs of garlic, and it requires no management after initial placement in the fall.

The drawbacks of fresh grass mulches are few. Finding the material at all may be the toughest problem since most garlic growers don't own their own orchards. Pasture grass is fine if it's weed free. Some growers can buy a cutting of fresh pasture grass from a small nearby landowner and make a deal to cut and haul the grass themselves rather than buy dried, baled hay. Others could collect grass clippings from lawns around town, but they need to be conscious of possible pesticide applications, weed seeds, and other contaminants.

It's a little tricky to apply the grass at exactly the right depth. When applied too thinly, it fails to suppress weed growth and also decomposes more rapidly than is desirable. If applied too thickly, you may have to help some garlic plants break through the mulch in early spring. There's an art and skill to applying a grass mulch at the right depth without thick lumps. Experience is the best teacher.

My second choice for mulch is old, chopped wheat straw. In the west, it's widely available at reasonable prices, very lightweight, and easy to haul. It's also easy to spread, providing it hasn't gotten wet and started to rot. In general, the lighter the color and the lighter the weight of the bale, the better the texture and the easier (it is to spread).

Chopped wheat straw has disadvantages. It's more liable to blow away in a strong wind when it's dry. It's light color reflects light and heat so that soil warms slowly in the spring. Straw is almost pure cellulose and will require the addition of a nitrogen source when it's turned into the soil after garlic harvest. Finally, straw has a large capacity to hold water and may require some management such as temporary removal to allow drying if a long wet spell results in a soggy topsoil, especially during the last four weeks before harvest. Chopped straw usually also contains some grain seeds that can attract mice, quail and deer—not normally a serious problem unless excessive mouse populations begin actually nesting in the straw. Some growers solve that problem by mulching over winter and then removing the mulch totally in May when bulbing begins.

We've had fantastic results in small areas by using well chopped deciduous leaves as a mulch. By May the leaf particles are decayed into a rich layer of pure humus alive with earthworms and worm castings. The garlic loves it. Unfortunately, leaf mulches may refuse to decay in cool wet climates; in fact, whole slimy leaves can result in anaerobic (airless) conditions at the soil surface.

At the risk of repeating myself, I'd like to emphasize that mulching is very much an art. We still feel that we get better at it every year. Don't be surprised, and don't give up, just because your first attempt turns out less than perfect. I can't recommend mulches highly enough. All plants in nature benefit from natural mulches as plant matter decays over winter. I see no reason to rob cultivated plants of the same benefits just because a bare cultivated soil is easier to manage.

The lesson is simple. Growers in the western and northern United States stand to gain immeasurably from good mulches on their garlic crops especially if only light snow cover is likely. Many growers in the Great Plains and Intermountain Northwest froze out in the winter of 1989-90 because of subzero temperatures, no snow, and no mulch. Eastern growers in more humid, temperate climates will have to manage mulches carefully, but the same potential benefits are always available.

Winter Journal Entries

November 29—Winter storm watch. The morning sky is slate-gray and ominous. The air feels damp and heavy, and the early morning temperature is a surprisingly mild thirty-six degrees Fahrenheit. Overcast skies during the night held in the little bit of heat generated by the previous day's sunshine. But, brisk winds are picking up rapidly, already gusting to twenty miles per hour.

The winds always come in advance of a weather front this time of year. Today's are from the south which means the actual front has not yet arrived. It's a low pressure system from the Gulf of Alaska. As it drops southward and eastward, its cold air will collide continually with the warmer air of the jet stream.

The Weather Service issued a high wind advisory late last night, predicting gusts up to fifty miles per hour— perhaps they'll blow the mulch off the garlic field. Up to four inches of rain are possible on the flood-weary coast and up to four feet of snow in the Cascades. This low pressure system has apparently been spinning counterclockwise in the Gulf for some time, building strength and picking up moisture.

But all the Weather Service predictions mean very little to me. Filaree Farm sits in the heart of a rain shadow that extends over the central populated portion of Okanogan County for about twenty miles both north and south of us. Due west, over both the Arlington Ridge and the Loup Loup Mountains, the Methow River valley is nestled at the base of the Cascade foothills. It steals more than ninety percent of the moisture intended for us, and it's undoubtedly raining (or snowing) there now.

The average annual precipitation at Filaree Farm in the ten years I've kept records is 14.49 inches, about three inches more per year than the old maps show for the long term average in the main Okanogan River valley. Either way, this is semi-arid, sagebrush steppe. The Okanogan valley is the northernmost finger of the great Columbia Basin steppe that is the heartland of eastern Washington and also the northern-most tip of a great desert/steppe that extends all the way south into Mexico. The majority of eastern Washington lies in the rain shadow of the Cascades, but Filaree Farm sits within an even more sheltered microclimate. It's not uncommon for rain or snow to fall heavily in the north, south, east, and west—only ten to twenty miles away—while not a drop falls here.

About eighty percent of our moisture falls as rains, primarily in the spring and fall. Winters have been very mild in recent years with very few arctic blasts and seldom more than six inches of snow on the ground at any one time. It hasn't exactly been the "far north" that most people imagine. The ten year trend is troubling since the water table has fallen significantly and isn't expected to rise unless we experience two or three winters in a row with a very heavy snowpack. The long range winter forecast for the Pacific Northwest was issued only two days ago. It calls for above average precipitation and above average temperatures. I expect the mild temperatures, but I'll be surprised to see much snow.

December 1—The garlic has good roots now. They extend between six and twelve inches deep depending on which week they were planted. None of the cloves show visible sprouts when the mulch and soil are brushed away, but dissected cloves show that early elongation of the leaf sprouts is well under way inside the clove. Soil temperatures have fallen from the low forties two weeks ago to the upper thirties this week. The forty to forty-five degrees temperatures in late October pretty much ended the garlics' state of rest, although Artichoke strains probably needed the extra two weeks in November to break their dormancy. The cooler temperatures of late November insured that growth would not be fast and furious, but growth has begun.

Significant leaf growth will not occur now until average soil temperatures climb back above forty degrees Fahrenheit next March. The sprout will survive until then on the food of its storage leaf (or clove). Root growth will continue all winter, as will leaf growth at a snail's pace. Only a deep freeze below the two inch soil depth would stop all growth and that, hopefully, will be quite temporary. The sprout, the true stem, and the roots will not be damaged unless they all freeze solid quite suddenly. That circumstance should be prevented by the mulch and the heat of the soil organic matter.

Last winter was one of the mildest in history. Temperatures climbed into the wonderful fifties and even the unbelievable sixties during January (normally our coldest month). Nearly half the garlic plants emerged from the mulch and grew despite frosty nights. It was in early January that I suddenly realized I had a rare opportunity to determine minimum threshold temperatures for garlic growth.

Now don't laugh. I never pretended to be a scientist. How would you measure the growth of garlic leaves if you were a typical garlic farmer? With a ruler, of course.

I first cut small square blocks of lathe and positioned them firmly in the soil at the base of the plants, ten ophio and ten sativum. Soil thermometers were placed at a two inch soil depth (i.e. at the base of the planted cloves) in two representative locations. Air temperatures were recorded on a battery operated temperature graph (my one piece of semi-sophisticated equipment) that showed the temperature at any given time of the day or night.

During the short days of January, all growth measurements were taken at noon. By early February, I began recording data three times a day, and by mid-February, I even added fifty more plants of five additional cultigens. The test took an interesting turn January 30th when it snowed six inches, but the snow was gone by February 11th. During that twelve day period, the tallest leaf on variety sativum had elongated an average one quarter inch, and variety ophioscorodon about forty percent less. Yet, a few individual plants had grown more than one half inch beneath the snow. Clearly, winter was no obstacle to growth!

By graphing the daily data for each individual plant, as well as the daily, weekly, and biweekly averages for each group of ten plants, I was able to paint a fairly accurate picture of garlic responses to a range of specific incidents; for instance, an arctic outbreak in mid-February. The results by the end of March were surprising.

Leaf growth on young garlic plants in fall, winter, and early spring appeared to be governed primarily by soil temperatures. Plants less than two inches in height were not even bothered by hard overnight frosts. But as the total exposed leaf surface area grew, so did the significance of the air temperature. On the other hand, when averaged over weekly periods, the average soil temperature was usually within two to three degrees of the average air temperature.

Garlic leaf growth occurs primarily at the base of the leaf (i.e. leaf tips do not elongate). Positive leaf growth as measured over any twenty-four hour period continued until overnight temperatures fell to approximately twenty-four to twenty-six degrees. Sativum garlic appeared to have a slightly lower minimum threshold temperature (about two degrees lower) than did ophio garlics. Garlic leaf tissues contract in cold air so I sometimes recorded negative growth. Nonetheless, I measured increases in leaf length between dusk and dawn repeatedly when evening temperatures dropped to near freezing within an hour of darkness, and below freezing shortly thereafter.

The data clearly showed that sativum garlics germinated and emerged more slowly than ophio garlics, but sativums grew much faster than ophios after emergence. Sativums were generally less affected by cold overnight temperatures between twenty-five to thirty-two degrees Fahrenheit than were ophio garlics, but sativums were more severely affected by each successive degree of cold than were ophios. When minimum overnight low temperatures fell below the minimum threshold temperatures of approximately twenty-four degrees Fahrenheit for sativums and twenty-six degrees for ophios, sativums were much more quickly and severely affected. In general, it appeared that while sativums were more tolerant of minor cold they had less overall cold hardiness.

Easily observed leaf growth rates of more than one-sixteenth inch per day did not occur until mean average soil temperatures were above forty degrees Fahrenheit. The youngest and, generally, the smallest plants grew at faster rates than the older, taller plants. Despite the faster growth rates of sativum garlics, their total average plant height remained shorter than that of the earlier germinated ophios until late March.

Positive leaf growth over periods of twenty-four and seventy-two hours were recorded for both sativum and ophio plant groups despite soil temperatures of thirty-one degrees Fahrenheit and continuously frozen soil surrounding the cloves to a depth of three inches. Sudden and severe cold spells did shock the plants, but when the cold increased gradually the plants were apparently able to accumulate more cold hardiness. I recorded positive growth of ophio garlic groups over twenty-four hour periods (without snow cover) despite overnight lows of six degrees Fahrenheit, frozen soils to a three inch depth, and an average ophio plant height of more than three inches of leaf above the mulch.

When the first foliage leaf was damaged or killed by hard frosts, the second foliage leaf replaced it, and so on. Plants did not appear to die unless there was damage to the true stem. Even root dieback was followed by the appearance of new root shoots. By mid-February, when the first foliage leaf of ophio garlics averaged about four inches from soil surface to leaf tip, the growth rates of the second foliage leaves began to surpass those of the first leaf. However, both leaves continued to grow, sometimes despite severe dieback of the leaf tips.

By March 1st, the second foliage leaf was actually longer than the first foliage leaf for both sativum and ophio garlics. Shortly thereafter, I began measuring growth rates for third foliage leaves as well. Data collection continued to the end of March by which time soil temperatures were well above forty degrees Fahrenheit and growth rates as high as one-half inch per day were recorded.

Summary

Garlic is tough stuff! Except during the most extreme periods, it continues leaf elongation and root growth all

winter long, even in temporarily frozen soil. Severe overnight frosts and short subzero arctic outbreaks are only
temporary setbacks in the determined process of winter
growth which occurs most steadily during periods of insu-
lating snow cover, even when foliage leaves are well
emerged above ground. Very few domesticated food
plants can survive such conditions, let alone continue
growth throughout the period.

We're on the verge of another winter now, and I can't
help but feel a bit nervous as I gaze across mulched fields
lying still and quiet beneath winter skies. I suppose all
farmers know the feeling. But I suppose the garlic will
survive and flourish again this winter despite all Nature's
surprises and all my thoroughly human anxieties. Indeed,
I don't seem to be psychologically prepared for real winter yet. But the garlic—it's just *ended* its period of natural
rest and *started* its season of growth.

My Little Clove

Oh, garlic bulb,
Oh, little cloves—
You never die,
but grow and regrow
and multiply
from original cells
of some ancient
Mother-Bulb;

Oh, human spirit—
You sometimes falter,
but never die,
as you grow and regrow
and multiply
from original dreams
of ancient Parents.

It's said that we pass on
our memories,
but I suspect
(that like these bulbs)
we are our ancient
memories.

How else could I see
myself so clearly
in body
and in soul
in my Child?

My Garlic Child
My Little Clove.

—Ron Engeland

Spring Tasks

Ah, springtime! Warm sun reflecting off melting snow. Swelling buds and a greening world. What a joy when the garlic field begins popping green little fingers through its blanket of mulch.

On the other hand...What a lot of work there suddenly is to do. Spring is always a busy time, but garlic growers know it can't be blamed on the garlic. Provided there is adequate soil moisture, garlic gets off to a very early spring start while other plants are still waking up, and requires surprisingly little care early on.

Fertilization

We start to foliar feed young garlic with fish nutrient sprays as soon as plants are about three inches tall. We use a 12 - 0.25 - 1 wettable powder at a rate of one to two pounds per acre, and we usually add one-half to three-quarters of a pound of Maxicrop (powdered kelp) to ensure a balanced full spectrum foliar feed. There are a number of kelp products on the market, but many experts seem to think that North Atlantic sea kelp (*Ascophyllum nodosum*) is the best. Kelp contains very minimal amounts of nitrogen, phosphorus, and potassium (which are supplied by the fish meal) but contains a large compliment of other elements including cytokinins, gibberellins, and auxins. There is, admittedly, debate about the effectiveness of kelp, especially when applied to soils as a dry meal, but we feel fairly certain that the foliar spray blend of fish and kelp provides cost-efficient sources of water soluble nutrients to the leaf surfaces where they are immediately available for plant use. Kelp is also said to impart cold hardiness in the early spring when hard frosts are still likely.

Our foliar nutrient sprays are applied at the rate of one hundred gallons of water per acre, so the mixed sprays are a one to two percent solution of fish and a one-half to three-quarter percent solution of kelp. The rates for gardeners would be approximately one and one-half ounces of dry fish powder per gallon of water per one thousand square feet of garlic, and two tablespoons of Maxicrop per gallon. The two percent solution of fish equals about one-quarter pound of actual nitrogen per acre with about one-half of it in water soluble form, one-sixth (or seventeen percent) in the form of ammonia, and one-third in a water insoluble form.

Obviously, the total actual nitrogen per acre or per plant in such a two percent solution is very minimal. This is a supplemental foliar feeding, not a heavy dose or a full years supply of nutrients; therefore, we assume a soil already nutrient balanced and healthy. We think the foliar feeding is more efficient than sidedressing of fertilizer because the nutrients are more immediately available to plants. In addition, less of the nutrients end up feeding weeds or leaching out of the soil profile.

One word of caution is in order, however. Some manufacturers suggest that the application of foliar nutrient sprays *during* periods of plant stress can give plants a quick boost. We think they can also severely shock the plants. Broad spectrum nutrient sprays (such as the fish and kelp combination) are best used preventitively rather than as a quick solution to a severe deficiency. Plants can be stressed (rather than relieved of stress) by the application of cold water onto warm leaf surfaces in the late afternoon sun, and also by the application of readily available water soluble nutrients when plants are stressed by lack of soil moisture. We think the foliar sprays work best if applied a day or two after an irrigation or a rainfall. Water stressed plants simply can't utilize abundant nutrients, so the abundance becomes, in effect, excess.

We try to apply foliar fish and kelp at two week intervals from mid-March through early May—three to four total applications. The usual plant response is an immediate deep blue-green leaf color. Plant leaves seem to suddenly stand taller as if with increased turgor and vigor.

A second caution. It's too late to apply foliar nutrient sprays to small, yellowish plants in the mounting heat of late May. Plants are done growing leaves by then, so they can't utilize abundant nutrients, especially nitrogen. Once again, seeming abundance turns to excess and interferes with normal plant functions (in this case, the process of bulbing).

Not everyone appreciates foliar nutrient feeding. I've heard people pooh-pooh such sprays as "unnecessary if you have healthy soil." Certainly, the foliar feeding can't take the place of good soil or even substitute much for inadequacies in soil nutrient availability. I think of the sprays like vitamin supplements—a little boost to top off an already healthy diet.

If you'd rather apply fertilizers to the soil, I recommend sidedressing along the rows or broadcasting onto bed plantings. Synthetic fertilizers must be applied very judiciously as they are highly water soluble and capable of burning plant roots. Most professionals recommend several moderate spring applications of highly mobile elements such as nitrogen at rates of twenty to thirty pounds actual nitrogen per acre per application.

I still prefer dried blood meal as an organic source of nitrogen that becomes available slowly over a one to six week period as it decomposes via natural soil processes. Regardless of the material, it should be applied in early to mid-spring rather than late, and it should not be applied to water-stressed plants.

We've also heard from a number of experienced growers who feel that garlic grown with relatively high amounts of rapidly available nitrogen, such as nitrate and ammoniacal forms, is liable to store very poorly compared to bulbs fertilized with more slowly available nitrogen from organic sources. There's been a long debate about whether or not the various forms of nitrogen have different effects on food plants. Organic growers often claim organic nitrogen is better. We feel strongly that nitrogen is nitrogen, but that *slowly available* nitrogen results in healthier plants with higher soluble solids. The various forms of nitrogen fertilizer are more significant in their effect on soil microorganisms and the availability of other soil nutrients than in the way their actual nitrogen is utilized by crop plants.

Bulbing plants are said to be heavy potassium feeders, but studies on garlic by University of California researchers showed no increases in yield from specific fertilization with potassium or phosphorus materials. These elements are considered immobile; that is, they don't move rapidly through the soil. It is, therefore, difficult to make up for specific deficiencies of these elements in the soil in the middle of the growing season, and they're best incorporated into soils prior to planting in the fall.

Garlic is a tough plant and an efficient user of nutrients, so don't overdo the fertilizer, especially the micronutrients which can easily reach toxic levels. An example is selenium which garlic accumulates more than most garden or food plants. Yet total selenium needs are quite small. I think garlic mines selenium from deep in the subsoil and brings it toward the surface through its roots, leaves, and bulb. Since much of the root system breaks off and remains to decay in the soil after harvest, there is the possibility that garlic crops can increase the total selenium in the top one foot of soil. Specific research would be interesting. (Note that some U.S. soils *are* selenium deficient.)

A good three year crop rotation that employs legumes, grasses, and broad-leaved plants should prevent serious deficiencies of minor nutrients. Certain crops accumulate certain elements more than others. For instance, cabbage family plants (brassicas) accumulate selenium. If you're convinced your soil is deficient in a specific micronutrient, try composting or green manuring the plants that are know accumulators of those micronutrients.

Irrigation

This section is written primarily for small-scale farmers in the western United States. I've been directly involved in either the installation or design of irrigation systems, both turf and agricultural, for twenty-four years. Much of my knowledge and love of soil/plant interactions was learned indirectly through irrigation experiences in the Midwest, Southwest, and Northwest. Very few eastern growers would even consider irrigating a pasture or a garlic field, but many Midwesterners began to understand the usefulness of this early agricultural innovation during droughts over the past decade. I actually designed and sold drip and micro systems for growers in Iowa, Minnesota, Michigan, and Kentucky a few years back during one of the more severe droughts. There simply weren't any irrigation companies or irrigation experts in the affected regions. Some growers signed two month waiting lists just to get advice about irrigation from Cooperative Extensions agents, after which there were still no local companies to buy irrigation systems from.

In much of the western United States, irrigation is, quite simply, the difference between life and death. I won't argue the complicated issues involved in turning thousands of acres of desert, steppe, and prairie into cultivated, irrigated farmland. Suffice it to say, if you own such a piece of land now, you have just as much responsibility to care for it as for the crops you grow on it.

Garlic is really two plants in one. The early spring garlic is a vigorous, green, leafy vegetable that benefits from ample moisture and nutrients like any other salad green or rapidly growing vegetative plant. Notice that I said "benefits," not "requires." Inadequate moisture in early spring won't kill garlic, but it will definitely reduce plant and bulb size. It's the total size and number of green leaves developed in spring that determine the size of the bulb later on.

It is possible to overirrigate garlic in early spring, but the watering schedule used for most leafy green vegetables in the garden won't be too much for garlic. On the other hand, many gardeners apply too much or too little water to their gardens, so let's review some basic ground rules.

A good garden soil is about fifty percent soil particles (mixtures of clay, sand, and silt particles), twenty-five percent air, and twenty-five percent soil solution (i.e. water and associated chemical compounds). Overirrigation reduces the percentage of air and waterlogs the soil as well as leaching mobile nutrients (like nitrogen) out of the topsoil. Underirrigation results in too much air, at least temporarily, but often ends up producing a compacted soil with very little air. Neither waterlogged nor dry airless soils are conducive to micro-organisms, nor can certain chemical reactions and processes of decomposition take place without the proper blend of water and air to act as chemical catalysts or as physical agents to transport materials.

Traditional irrigation systems apply large amounts of water, rapidly filling the soil to its maximum water holding capacity. If irrigation continues beyond this point then excess water either runs off the surface or is pulled straight down and out of the soil by the force of gravity. When irrigation stops, water seeks to distribute itself evenly throughout the soil. Then moisture levels begin to slowly decline due to use and evaporation at the surface plant.

Sandy soils with very little soil organic matter lose most of their available moisture in only three to five days. Sandy loams (with larger amount of silt and clay) take six to ten days to achieve significant drying. Heavier clay soils can retain water for up to twenty days. Of course, these cycles (wet to dry) get stretched out in cool weather and shortened up in hot weather. Once dry, the irrigation system is turned back on and the soil again saturated.

This traditional cycling of soil moisture levels from one extreme to the other is certainly less than ideal. It may mean that plants spend nearly one-quarter of their lives struggling to grow in soils that are temporarily too wet or too dry. Good managers, who know their soil type, its water holding capacity, and the amount of water applied by their irrigation system, can avoid the extremes somewhat so that moisture levels are usually in the range of fifty percent to ninety percent available moisture. That's a decent range within which plants can grow without stress. When more than half the soil moisture is gone (i.e. less than fifty percent available moisture) plants have to spend more time and energy searching for moisture and nutrients. They also have to work harder to utilize the nutrients they do find. A little extra work challenges the plant, but too much "forced labor" weakens the plant and reduces yields.

How do you know when the fifty percent level is reached? The time honored method is to brush aside the top few inches of soil and grab a handful of earth. Form it into the shape of a round ball. If the ball is muddy or soggy or slimy then the soil is too wet. If you can't even form a ball because the dry soil crumbles, then soil is too dry. Anything in between is okay. This method is fast, simple, and cheap. It's worked for centuries, so why not try it?

There are also more technical and precise methods. I use tensiometers at six inch and eighteen inch soil depths. They consist of a gauge and a small water reservoir on top of a plastic tube with a ceramic tip on the bottom. Tensiometers function exactly like mechanical roots and tell you almost exactly how hard plant roots are having to work to extract moisture from soil particles. The gauge readings translate roughly into the percentage of available soil moisture. A reading of "seventy-five" indicates approximately seventy-five percent of available soil moisture is still present.

Tensiometers require distilled water. Once installed and filled the operator pumps a vacuum on the gauge and screws on the lid. When soil is wet, moisture passes into the tube through the ceramic tip and raises the gauge reading towards "one hundred" or saturation. As soil dries, water leaves the tube and lowers the gauge reading. Tensiometers may cost forty to fifty dollars each and provide most accurate information when installed in pairs—one shallow and one deep. Paired instruments tell you not only the amount of moisture, but how deep your irrigations are penetrating into the soil, and whether or not your subsoil is drying out despite a wet topsoil. These convenient tools allow careful managers to maintain soil moisture levels between any two chosen levels simply by changing the length of the irrigation or the frequency between irrigations.

Innovations in irrigation in the last twenty years include drip and micro systems. Both systems can conserve water if properly managed. They can also apply water more efficiently than large impact sprinklers and they operate at much lower pressures.

Both drip and micro systems are based on the premise that by applying smaller amounts of water more frequently, we can avoid the extremes of wet and dry and maintain near constant optimum conditions for plant growth. But that's where the similarities end.

Micro sprinklers are low volume, low pressure plastic sprinklers generally costing between seventy-five cents and one dollar twenty-five cents each. They throw or deflect water in an eight to fourteen foot radius, and they are seldom spaced farther than twenty feet apart from each other in any direction. When well-spaced at about fifty-five percent of the diameter of throw, they distribute water more uniformly than impact sprinklers. The finer droplet sizes are ideal for seed germination, and they don't bombard the soil or splash mud on plants. Micros typically operate at fifteen to thirty pounds of pressure and can be mounted on PVC pipe, poly pipe, or on hose sleds.

Drip systems don't throw or spray water. Rather, water drips or dribbles out of very tiny orifices onto specific points of application. There is a wet spot on the soil surface, but as the water penetrates into the soil it spreads out in a circle with a possible radius of about four feet in heavy soil or one foot in light sandy soil. Soil surfaces largely remain dry despite amply wetted soil in the plant root zone. Weed seed germination and weed growth are greatly reduced and so are evaporative losses from the soil surface. Row crops or beds require emitters every twelve to eighteen inches and lateral distribution lines every three to six feet to insure a uniformly wet root zone. Most drip lines are made out of ultra-violet resistant polyethylene that doesn't deteriorate rapidly in sunlight. Unfortunately, they usually require chlorination to prevent eventual algae growth that clogs up the tiny emitter orifices.

We irrigate garlic with micro sprinklers in the spring and switch to drip lines in mid to late May when the weather turns hot and the garlic starts to bulb. The drip system allows us to begin drying out the soil surface before harvest so maturing bulbs aren't as susceptible to molds and fungi. Drip also minimizes weed growth during the period when our grass mulch is nearly decayed and no longer substantial enough to suppress weed seed germination.

Our irrigation system is probably deluxe compared to most growers' systems, but it's also portable; that is, we move both the PVC micro lines and the poly drip lines across the fields in about five days time so that the system cost is only one-fifth that of a permanent system.

The trickiest question when irrigating garlic is when to stop prior to harvest. By cutting water off too early, we force early maturity, rapid drydown, and early harvest—often resulting in smaller bulbs that harden off poorly and don't store well. But if we keep watering too long, we run the risk of diseases, molds, stained bulb wrappers, and even rotting bulbs. The drip system allows us to maintain adequate moisture in the root zone without water logging the topsoil. That greatly reduces the risk of most of the aforementioned problems. We still start tapering off the water in June as soon as the flower stalks have formed their curls on the ophio garlics. Our last irrigation is generally about two weeks before harvest.

Of course, nature always seems to surprise us with at least one rainfall after our last irrigation. We've almost suffered damage from botrytis neck rot in years when serious drenchings occurred, but our semi-arid climate normally dries soil surfaces rapidly. Eastern growers may well want to stop irrigating earlier if there is a high probability of rainfall prior to harvest. In fact, if eastern growers irrigate at all, they are likely to use irrigation systems supplementally with no more than one or two irrigations per year.

If you're growing garlic commercially and you need to irrigate, I highly recommend you seek the advice of an expert rather than watering by the seat of your pants. (That's when you sit down in the soil to see how wet it is.) Improper irrigation can ruin a good soil as well as a good garlic crop.

Warning Signs

The "what to look for" part is easy. The first warning sign from garlic is almost always yellowing leaves. The "how to determine the cause" part is more difficult and requires careful investigation of more subtle details.

The time of year is sometimes an important clue, although nutrient deficiencies can show up at any time after about thirty days from emergence (approximately when the old clove is no longer supplying any nutrients to the young plant). Yellowing leaves in very early spring often indicate penicillium molds. If just the leaf tips turn yellow (or burnt brown) but not the rest of the leaf, it's most likely frost damage or a minor nutrient deficiency. Minor nutrient deficiencies are nothing to panic about; in fact, they're usually the result of a soil imbalance of nutrients rather than an actual soil deficiency. It is important to keep an eye on plants with yellow tips to see if the yellow areas increase in size or if the plants develop additional symptoms.

The truth is yellow leaf tips are very common in most of the garlic fields I've seen. Only highly fertile soils seem free of them—and then only in most years. We've conducted lots of experiments to try and determine a specific cause, but to no avail. The best I can tell you is yields don't seem to be seriously reduced.

Yellowing of whole leaves in April or May is more likely to indicate a serious disease or a serious water or nutrient deficiency. Carefully remove a few affected plants and bulbs and study them for further clues. Are the roots also affected? Is the plant rotting at the base? Is the stem slimy? Where are the affected plants located? Is it a few random isolated plants, or a group of adjacent plants? Does the affected area grow in size?

Random plants seldom indicate a serious problem. It's more likely a damaged clove or a weak plant. Even a large group of yellowing plants in a specific area could be caused by a drainage problem, a careless overdose of fertilizer, or a plugged sprinkler rather than a disease or nutrient deficiency. If plants are seriously yellowed, we remove and destroy them whether we can pinpoint the cause or not. There's no good reason to leave a sick plant in the middle of a healthy field.

Late season yellowing may have any number of causes, but don't confuse it with normal plant maturation in which leaves begin turning yellow or brownish from the leaf tips downward, and also from the bottom of the plant (oldest leaves) upward toward the youngest leaves.

Flavio Couto did a somewhat famous study of deficiency symptoms in garlic in 1955 while working on his Master of Science at the University of California at Davis. The results of his findings are summarized briefly in the chart on page 118. Deficiency symptoms for phosphorus are not included in the chart because they are not distinctive and vary from plant to plant. In general, they closely resemble the symptoms of nitrogen deficiency except that young leaves do not fold and grow in a loop as they have a slight tendency to do when nitrogen is deficient.

The symptoms of boron deficiency in garlic are also not shown in the chart because they are so distinctive. According to Couto, the first symptom is an outbending of the lower leaves, especially the third, fourth, and fifth leaves. The newer leaves above these form close together and appear more upright than normal and somewhat disassociated from the lower leaves. General chlorosis, or yellowing of leaves, begins in the youngest leaves and soon effects all the upright leaves at the top of the plant. In more advanced stages, purplish veins begin appearing at the leaf tips of the medium aged leaves. The purpling moves downward in the leaves until the entire plant may have a slightly purplish look. Then leaf tips begin to die back. In severe cases, the mature cloves of the bulb may be wet and soft—when cut in cross-section the cloves may have white, corky patches of deteriorated flesh.

Element	First Signs	Oldest or Youngest Leaves Affected First	Leaf Tip or Base First	New Leaves After First Symptoms Appear	Symptoms In Later Stages
Nitrogen	yellow leaf tips	oldest	tip	Continue to be produced with normal color, but each new leaf smaller so plant looks stunted	Purple veins at base of upper leaf blades and throughout lower leaf sheaths.
Potassium	deep yellow leaf tips	oldest	tip	Small and weak with fewer total leaves than in normal plants	General chlorosis of upper leaf blade. Deep yellow at leaf tip starts at margin and moves in and down. Complete yellowing and death of older leaves occurs rapidly.
Calcium	necrotic spots	all	upper one-third of upper leaf blade	none	As spots increase in size, the leaf blade bends down and leaf tips die. Gradual dieback of entire leaf. About one-half as many total leaves as a normal plant. May produce rounds instead of cloved bulbs.
Magnesium	general chlorosis	oldest	base	Continue to be produced with normal color. Sharp contrast with older, yellow leaves.	Often only three to five green leaves at any time. Lower leaves yellow or dead.

Table 1. Comparison of Some Deficiency Symptoms in Garlic (adapted from F. Couto, 1956)

Pests and Diseases

The incidence of pest and disease problems encountered by garlic growers is a function of several key factors. Generally speaking,

- the wetter the climate, the higher the occurrence of most diseases and many pests
- the closer you are located to a commercial onion/garlic growing area, the higher the likelihood of problems
- both of the above factors become irrelevant if you purchase and plant infected planting stock in the first place
- all three of the above factors can be minimized with good planting stock, healthy soil care, good crop rotations, and careful sanitary measures

The last factor, human management, is by far the most important. Even isolated growers in the far north can encounter problems—no locations in North America are immune—but good growers can overcome most challenges before they turn into disasters.

Most states and countries with commercial Allium industries (e.g. California and Washington, the United States and Canada) require phytosanitary certificates proving that planting stock is free from stem and bulb nematode and white rot before the stock may be shipped into those regions. Most of these areas actually have legal quarantines in effect.

If you are lucky enough to live within a quarantine area, the state will usually conduct automatic annual inspections for a small fee. The purpose is to protect that state's Allium industry. If you don't live within a quarantine area, the state automatically assumes your garlic has **all** the major pests and diseases. Small individual growers cannot legally ship garlic planting stock without paying the cost of expensive tests for all the major pests and diseases **every year**. The cost is obviously prohibitive for most small growers; thus, there is an actively flourishing trade in illegally shipped garlic planting stock in America. It's one more example of regulations so restrictive that small growers are forced to ignore the law in order to survive. Most of the small growers I know would like to be inspected, but, until the fees become more reasonable, small growers must rely on their own knowledge and instincts, and on the assumed integrity and knowledge of the people they're buying from.

Stem and Bulb Nematode

The most damaging pest in commercially grown garlic in America is the Stem and Bulb Nematode (*Ditylenchus dipsaci*). The nematode is a very small organism, somewhat worm-like, and normally too small to be seen with the naked eye. It commonly attacks onions and garlic, but may attack all members of the Onion Family as well as the Shasta Pea (*Pisum sativum*), parsley (*Petroselinum crispum*), celery (*Apium graveolens*), and salsify (*Tragopogon porrifolius*).

Once introduced, the stem and bulb nematode persists in the soil for many years. Crop rotations and sanitary measures are extremely important in controlling this organism since no chemical, biological, or cultural controls are known. Never plant any of the known host plants before or after an onion or garlic crop, and don't allow volunteer plants or nearby weed patches (such as salsify). We never spread garlic stems or bulb wrappers back onto the field. Instead we compost them thoroughly, or we burn them. Even after composting we're careful not to spread the compost on any of the garlic fields.

In the field, lightly infested garlic plants show no symptoms. The first signs of a serious problem are often stunted plants with pale, thickened leaves that soon become twisted, rolled, or obviously stunted in shape. The organism actually invades the tissue of the stem. When infestations are severe (usually mid to late season), the bottom portion of the plant becomes swollen and spongy. Vertical cracks or splits may occur in the region where the bulb would eventually occur. By the time leaves look obviously twisted and stunted, there is usually rot and decay of the lower stem tissues. The basal plate (or true stem) may break away and remain in the soil if the plant is pulled from the ground. Since severe stunting may occur fairly rapidly, it's almost impossible to avoid serious yield reductions.

Most of the nematodes remain in the plant tissues rather than the soil, so infected plants should be carefully dug—not pulled—from the ground and destroyed by burning. Early detection and careful disposal is the second line of defense—obviously not as desirable as purchase of clean planting stock in the first place.

Nematodes may also remain dormant for long periods in both the soil and in cull garlic and harvest litter before seeking out a new host.

The stem and bulb nematode can occasionally be transported via onion seed, but garlic bulbs are one of the chief means of introduction. Some cultigens appear semi-resistant (such as California Early), but none are completely immune. Serious yield reductions on all cultigens will result if this pest goes undetected very long.

Onion Thrips

This insect pest may surpass the stem and bulb nematode in the worldwide damage it causes, despite the fact that direct controls are available. The onion thrip (*Thrips tabaci*) is slender, about one twenty-fifth of an inch long (1 to 1.2 mm) and usually light brown in color. Adults have two pair of fringed wings and fly great distances. Both adults and larvae attack plant leaves by sucking juices. Injured areas turn white or silvery from the lack of chlorophyll. Damage first appears as small spots that eventually run together to form large areas. Entire fields may appear silvery in severe infestations.

The life cycle of the onion thrip is very short, about two to three weeks, so up to ten generations per year are possible. Only three to four generations are likely in northern, cold winter regions since this insect slows its activities significantly in cool weather, yet the rapidity of its life cycle remains the primary obstacle to control. Hard rains (even sprinkler irrigation) can actually kill onion thrips, but eggs and young larvae (white or pale yellow) are usually found on inner leaves near the base of the plant where they are well protected. Growing larvae molt twice and reach maturity within five days of hatch in warm weather. Mature larvae enter the soil to pupate (the only time during the life cycle that they enter the soil). Pupation may last up to one week, but adults often emerge from the soil in about four days when temperatures are warm.

Onion thrips vary in severity annually depending on climate and rainfall. They are most active in warm weather and most severe in dry years. They can use various grasses and weeds as alternate hosts, so weed control on nearby land is important. They hibernate and overwinter in almost any protected places including inside the garlic bulb wrappers during storage.

Serious infestations of onion thrip may require chemical control when larvae are still young. Coverage of the lower plant in the leaf axils is important. Fish oil, when used as a spreader-sticker agent at a relatively high two to three percent rate with foliar nutrient sprays, should provide some control. (Fish oil is not registered as a pesticide.) Don't apply fish oil when temperatures exceed ninety degrees Fahrenheit or when freezing may occur before the oil dries, nor under windy conditions that cause rapid drying and volatilization, nor within thirty days of any sulphur based materials. Remember, also, that fish oil provides some nutrient benefit.

Safer's Insecticidal Soap is fairly effective against some kinds of thrips at early stages of growth, but it's not registered for use on Alliums specifically, and has not been tested on onion thrip.

Traditional chemical controls are available. Consult a licensed professional, and always follow label instructions precisely.

There is a predatory mite (*Amblyseius cucumeris*) that specifically attacks onion thrips and Western flower thrips. It is very tiny, tan colored, and less than 0.5 mm in length, but it moves very quickly to capture its prey. If it succeeds in eliminating all the thrips, it will often remain at the site feeding on pollen, leaf surface fungi, or spider mite eggs. Unfortunately for growers in the western U.S., this predatory mite thrives in high humidity and is most useful in the greenhouse. Most pesticides are harmful to it.

Ladybug and syrphid fly larvae also readily attack onion thrips during the immature stages of the pest's life cycle.

Mites

Several mites can attack garlic, especially stored bulbs, but serious economic losses do not appear to be common. The eriophyid mite (*Aceria tulipae*) is a frequent pest that can damage bulbs stored for long periods. The mite is too small to be seen even with a hand lens. It injures very young leaves before they emerge from the clove, but growing plants usually recover even when mites are abundant in the folds of leaves.

Northern growers should have very little to fear from the eriophyid mite, especially since they plant in the fall (i.e. no long bulb storage). Southern growers may see slow emergence from the soil. Young plants may have distorted, twisted leaves with yellow or light green streaks, yet these plants often appear normal by midseason. I recommend removal and destruction of individual plants with obvious yellow streaked or twisted leaves.

Onion Maggot

While often a serious pest of onions, shallots, and chives, the onion maggot (*Hylemya antiqua*) seems to attack garlic less frequently than almost any other Allium. Except in a few regions, most growers consider the maggot only a minor pest. Nevertheless, onion maggot is so common in gardens that the pest may appear at any time, and garlic growers should at least be prepared to recognize and control the pest.

The onion maggot is an adult fly, grayish, slender, and

resembling a small housefly. The maggot overwinters in the pupal stage either a few inches deep in the soil or in cull onions and garlic. Flies emerge in spring and soon mate. Females lay thirty to forty eggs each at the base of plants or in the soil. Eggs are white and elongated. Hatch occurs in only three to eight days.

Young maggots are translucent white, legless, and about one millimeter long. They migrate to the plants, bore into the underground stem and then down into the bulb (if late in the season). Young garlic plants yellow, wilt and die. Maturing plants turn yellow but may not die until bulbs are completely hollowed out. A very strong odor accompanies rot due to bacteria carried on the maggots. The maggots look almost identical to cabbage maggot and seed corn maggot, but they only attack Alliums. They continue feeding until they become one-quarter to three-eighths of an inch long and a dirty white color. This may take from fifteen to twenty-five days. Maggots grow faster in warm, moist weather and slower in cool, dry weather.

When feeding is finished, the maggots pupate in the soil or in plant litter, usually several inches beneath the soil surface. The pupa is elongated, usually reddish or yellowish-brown with blunt, rounded ends, and somewhat resembling a large kernel of wheat. Overwintering pupae may be black in color. Pupation during the summer lasts one to two weeks before the adult fly emerges.

Light infestations of onion maggot can be controlled by hand removal of the yellowed plants which must be burned or buried more than one foot deep. Chemical controls are rarely necessary on garlic except in areas of large commercial production where crops are not rotated.

In northern regions, the maggots seldom appear until late in the season, about three to five weeks before harvest, except in coastal regions where winters are very mild. While serious infestations are rare in my region, I do know of one grower with one acre of garlic who hand culled more than 5% of the crop in July and still had an excellent harvest.

Oddly enough, I've never found maggots in our garlic, but if I plant onions we usually find a few. Therefore, if the maggot is a problem in your garlic, I suggest planting onions (or shallots) as a trap crop a short distance from the garlic. Adult flies can also be trapped.

Army Worms

There are many strains of Army worms, all similar and all very cyclic in that they may appear in large numbers for one or two years, then disappear for five to ten years. The Salt-Marsh Caterpillar *(Estigmene acrea)* is very similar.

Young caterpillars are often hairy and grey. Mature caterpillars vary but are often black with yellow bands. All such caterpillars feed on a wide variety of green plants and may appear suddenly in large numbers when they migrate en masse from a depleted food source to a new site. They rarely present a problem in garlic since they appear just before the bulbs mature, at a time when the garlic has already finished its green leafy growth. The caterpillars begin feeding at the leaf tips, often skeletonizing the top portion of the leaf, but seldom eating enough to damage the plant before they pupate in the soil.

If caterpllars start chewing the upper leaf tips earlier in the season and there is a large population, then some control (enough to slow them down) can be obtained with any pesticide that controls leaf-eating caterpillars. An organically acceptable material is the Kurstaki strain of *Bacillus thuringiensis*. The bacillus is a live bacterial spore that is completely harmless to all living things except caterpillars. The bacillus must be ingested by the caterpillar which then gradually becomes sick and usually dies within two to three days. Unfortunately, the bacillus is not highly effective in hot weather (over ninety degrees Fahrenheit) as the spores are killed. In that case, two applications two to three days apart may be needed.

Wireworms

Wireworms of the genus *Limonius* may attack garlic bulbs, especially in fields which recently grew sod. The wireworm is the larval stage of the Click Beetle, a hard-shelled, yellow or brown beetle from one-half to one and a half inches long. The larval stage may damage garlic roots or bulbs in the field.

Soils known to have wireworms are simply poor choices for garlic fields. Turn sods into the soil a minimum one full year before planting garlic and grow rapid green manure crops so that fields are frequently cultivated. Allow fields to dry between crops if possible so the larvae have a dry environment with little or no food.

There is a predatory nematode (*Steinernema feltiae*, also know as *Neoaplectana carpopapsae*) that attacks more than two hundred and fifty soil inhabiting insects including wireworms and onion maggots. The nematode is applied in a water spray at the base of the crop plants. The soil should be irrigated beforehand, and soil temperatures must be at least sixty degrees Fahrenheit. Results vary widely depending on specific site conditions and the quantity applied. A minimum ten million nematodes are required for approximately every two hundred square feet of crop ground, and the nematodes are most effective when placed at specific sites (e.g. the base of plants). Billions of nematodes are needed for broadcast applications. If used at all, I recommend using predatory nematodes the year before garlic is planted. Growers applying the predator in late spring to nearly mature garlic crops should not expect any miracles. The nematodes may cost about $1.50 per million for small quantity orders, or as cheap as 25¢ per million when ordered by the billions.

White Rot

If the stem and bulb nematode is the most feared pest of garlic because no direct controls are known then White Rot (*Sclerotium cepivorum*) is the most feared disease organism—not only is no direct control known, but the causal organism may persist in soils for more than ten years even though no Allium crops are grown.

White Rot is most active at temperatures of fifty to sixty-eight degrees Fahrenheit. It is inhibited at temperatures above seventy-five degrees Fahrenheit. The disease occurs for longer periods of the season in the south and in coastal areas. In the north it may attack in spring before the weather turns hot.

Both leaf bases and roots are attacked. First symptoms are (take a wild guess) yellow leaves and die back of the leaf tips. Roots are eventually destroyed; thus, tops also die back and somewhat watery decay of the lower stem or bulb occurs, followed by complete rotting. White fluffy mycelium may be present, but "sclerotia" also form. These are hard, black, round bumps either on the surface or within the tissue. The fungus overwinters as the hard sclerotia which begin growth when temperatures warm up in the spring. Infections may persist (either active or dormant) on stored bulbs, but the fungus primarily attacks field garlic.

Nearly all states and countries with Allium industries require inspections and phytosanitary certificates asserting imported planting stock is free of White Rot fungus. The transport of a few lightly infested bulbs can easily escape detection by growers and laypersons.

Prevention is clearly the best solution. Crop rotation and cleanup of harvest litter can reduce the effect of established infestations, but only time can fully cure the problem once it is introduced.

Basal Rot

Basal Rot or "bottom rot" is caused by a *Fusarium* fungus—*Fusarium oxysporum*. *Fusarium* is a soil born fungus often described as a secondary invader because it attacks plants already damaged or weakened by bruising, cultivating, maggots, another disease, or any injury that ruptures cell walls and provides an easy point of entry.

Fusarium symptoms are nearly identical to those of White Rot except the rate of decay and dieback is usually slower. *Fusarium* is active at much higher temperatures than White Rot, so it's more likely to become evident late in the growing season during hot weather. Because of the slow rate of infection at cool temperatures, plants may be attacked in mid-spring yet continue to grow until harvest. Or, under good conditions, plants may die within two weeks of infection.

During storage, *Fusarium oxysporum* is most active at or above room temperatures. Lightly infested plants carried into storage will decay and dry until cloves have been reduced to shrivelled mummies. Storage decay can occur very rapidly at sixty-eight degrees Fahrenheit although drying and mummification may not occur rapidly unless temperatures are above eighty degrees Fahrenheit.

Fusarium can be avoided by crop rotation, sanitation, maintenance of healthy plants, and careful cullage during planting stock selection and clove popping.

Pink Root

Pink Root is caused by the fungus *Pyrenochaeta terrestris*. This is another warm weather disease that is most active at about seven-five to eighty-five degrees Fahrenheit. The fungus attacks nearly all Alliums but also has many other hosts so that uninfected garlic can become infected even in soils that have never grown Alliums. If all host plants are destroyed, the fungus may persist in soils one to three years; a three to four year rotation can eliminate the fungus.

Pink Root attacks only the roots of garlic. As roots turn pink, shrivel, and die, the plant commonly sends out new roots which, in turn, are soon infected. Affected plants are not usually killed, but yields are reduced and side cloves sometimes formed. The only above ground symptom is dieback of leaf tips. Pink colored roots are the obvious key to identification. Chemical controls are rarely applied.

Botrytis

Botrytis, also known as "neck rot," can apparently be caused by three different species of Botrytis, but *Botrytis allii* (or "grey-mold neck rot") is the most common. This fungus can be highly destructive to stored onions but only occasionally attacks garlic.

Neck Rot infection occurs in the field, usually within a few weeks of harvest. It is possible for infection to occur without any symptoms showing until after bulbs are in storage. Infection usually requires a combination of heat and prolonged periods of wetness near the soil surface. In severe cases, the stem becomes slimy and water-soaked. Garlic tops may pull off when harvest is attempted.

Botrytis occurs most frequently in maritime climates and in the more humid eastern United States. A combination of prolonged rain and soggy mulch presents ideal conditions, especially if temperatures are warm or hot. Softneck garlics are more susceptible to infection than are ophio garlics. Under moist conditions the fungus will continue to spread and whole bulbs may be rotted. Rapid drying and dry storage stop the spread. Most of the fungus may be removed from lightly infested bulbs during cleaning, but these bulbs should not be used as planting stock. Dry foliage and good air circulation in the field and in storage are the best prevention and the best cure. Drip irrigation is strongly recommended in areas with Botrytis problems.

Penicillium Molds

Clove rot in both stored and planted garlic may be caused by the very common fungus *Penicillium corymbiferum* which spreads primarily in storage, especially during handling and clove popping. The fungus spreads by means of air born spores. Though I've never personally experienced more than incidental infections, a neighbor of mine once lost over twenty thousand plants (100% of his crop).

In field garlic, penicillium attacks freshly planted stock in warm climates, or freshly emerged spring plants in cold winter climates. In some cases, fall infection leads to winterkill. If not killed then, young plants often turn yellow and weak shortly after emergence, and the cloves in the soil exhibit typical blue-green mold. In storage, too, the fleshy part of the clove is affected.

Penicillium infestations are typically the result of a small number of infected bulbs which contaminate a large number of cloves each with a small number of spores as bulbs are popped apart for planting. If the storage temperature for several weeks prior to planting was in the forty to fifty degree Fahrenheit range and soil conditions are right for rapid emergence, then young plants can often outgrow the penicillium and produce crops with only slight declines in productivity. More serious infestations may, however, spread from the planted cloves into the true stem (i.e. basal plate) and kill the garlic plants outright. Spreading from plant to plant in the soil is relatively rare, but spores travel easily prior to and during planting.

Most fungicides will control penicillium mold, but most are not registered for use on garlic as a pre-planting treatment of cloves. In California, a hot water/formaldehyde treatment was reported to reduce the incidence of mold. Organic farmers have fewer choices. Elemental sulphur is one of the few materials with fungicidal properties that is allowed in certified organic production, and its main benefits are from preventative applications. Kelp is also believed to have fungicidal properties. Though I've never heard of anyone trying it, cloves could conceivably be soaked five minutes in a light kelp tea before planting. (If you try it, please experiment on a small batch of cloves first.) I've also heard of dusting cloves with bone meal prior to planting, and that sounds like the cheapest, safest preventative measure.

In arid regions of the western United States, several growers claim to have controlled penicillium shortly after planting or in early spring with a heavy irrigation. The fungus is primarily a problem in stored garlic where conditions are relatively dry, and high moisture levels in the soil are known to suppress the fungus. It should be pointed out, however, there are several types of molds, and growers in the eastern United States may be troubled by molds that are actually encouraged by moist conditions.

The best protection (as always) is prevention. Select planting stock carefully. Don't pry apart obviously soft, rotting, or decaying bulbs in an attempt to save a few good cloves. You may infect lots of already popped cloves in the process. If you discover any kind of grey, blue, green, orange, or red mold on garlic, dispose of the bulb carefully and immediately—don't pass it around for inspection, and don't throw it into a food grade cull box for cosmetic culls. Wash your hands, or even change your clothes if you think you have spores on them.

If you suspect a fair percentage of your planting bulbs are infected, use them as table stock and get new, uninfected stock. Spores may be carried on the outer bulb wrappers of otherwise sound bulbs, so the penicillium cannot be *totally* avoided through bulb selection; however, the potential for serious infestations can be greatly reduced. Remember that *Penicillium corymbiferum* is primarily carried on the bulb and cloves—not in the soil.

No field treatments will be as effective in controlling penicillium as will care and attention in selecting uninfected planting stock. Healthy, organically alive soil can actually neutralize molds. This happens if the molds are rapidly attacked and destroyed by other beneficial microorganisms at the same time young garlic plants are growing vigorously enough to outgrow the penicillium.

Viruses

"Virus" is a somewhat terrifying term to farmers because so little is known about viruses. They're difficult to identify in the first place—somewhat like an invisible plague—and no simple controls (such as spraying) are possible.

Ironically, many researchers report that *all* cultivated garlics in existence carry viruses. Researchers in at least three countries (U.S.A., Canada, and the Soviet Union) have reportedly produced "virus free" garlic during the last decade by means of "tissue culture." The process of tissue culture is not really new, but it's only recently been applied to garlic. It involves removal of germ tissue from the clove. The tissue can be cultured in a controlled environment in order to propagate hundreds of new plants in a very short time.

We're still not clear how the process of tissue culture allows virus free garlic stock. Indeed, we've been taught for years that viruses are systemic. But, the viruses in question apparently do not invade the fundamental genetic structure of garlic.

The hope of virus free stock via tissue culture promises higher yields from our domesticated garlics, but both the process and the results are still somewhat speculative. We heard second hand of an Oregon researcher who claimed all his virus free stock produced gigantic bulbs three to five inches in diameter—so big he was unable to market the bulbs and abandoned his project.

No doubt we'll all be hearing more about tissue culture and propagation of virus free garlic planting stock in the near future. All we know for sure is most viruses appear to have only minimal effects on garlic yields.

Yellow Dwarf Virus

At least one virus which attacks Alliums, including garlic, is Yellow Dwarf Virus. It is reported to be worldwide in distribution and particularly troublesome among vegetatively propagated Alliums such as garlic, shallots, and potato onions. Severe epidemics have been reported in commercial Allium producing areas, especially where large amounts of culls or harvest litter are commonly dumped in a central location rather than composted, burned, or buried.

The first symptoms of Yellow Dwarf Virus are short yellow streaks at the base of freshly emerged leaves, not necessarily the first leaves early in the season. If the planting stock is infected, then the first leaf of the new plant may show the symptom, but plants may become infected during the season as the result of aphids, thrips, or even mechanical cultivation. Once infected, all subsequent leaf growth shows symptoms, but leaves developed before infection apparently remain free of the virus and never show symptoms. As a result, the overall effect of the virus on yields will vary significantly depending on the number of infected plants and the time of the season infection occurs. In addition, several different strains of the virus have been isolated with some reportedly very mild and others quite severe. No doubt, some garlic strains are less affected than others.

After infection, the yellow streaked leaves turn completely yellow and even crinkled depending on the susceptibility of the garlic strains, the strength of the viral strain, and the growing conditions. Stressed garlic plants are far more susceptible. There is even speculation that many garlics may carry mild strains of Yellow Dwarf Virus without ever showing noticeable symptoms unless plants are severely stressed by drought and heat, or by winter injury. Severe symptoms may include decidedly dwarfish plants, completely yellowed or pale yellow-green leaves, and twisted, distorted leaves and flower stalks. Small bulbs, often with secondary side cloves or sprouts, result from severe infections, but mild infections occurring late in the season may not reduce yields at all.

Yellow Dwarf Virus can be greatly reduced in significance by burning or deep burying all harvest litter and culls, and by controlling insects such as thrips and aphids in the field. Avoid the use of sprouted planting stock if aphids or thrips are found in the stock.

We still don't know of a cheap, easy test to verify the presence of Yellow Dwarf Virus, and mildly infected plants may produce the same slight yellowing of leaves that nearly any other form of stress, disease, or insect attack would produce. We don't know of any state with easily accessible testing facilities for garlic viruses.

If you suspect Yellow Dwarf Virus, we recommend careful isolation of the affected plants. Good quality bulbs can still be sold as table stock, but should not be allowed to contact planting stock. During harvest and cleaning, tools should be disinfected before use on the rest of the crop. A strong disinfectant is required—not simple bleach—and is usually available from greenhouse and nursery supply companies. Burning is the best way to destroy infected plant parts.

Pre-Harvest

We've already determined that the size and quality of the developing garlic bulb depends on the health and vigor of the plant earlier in the season. Overall quality, however, is probably more dependent on decisions made during the final month before harvest. Good management is still required to harden off the plant and harvest bulbs that look nice and store long enough to make it to market.

Popping Tops

Subspecies *ophioscorodon* garlics normally produce a false seedstalk topped by an umbel enclosing small aerial bulbils. Most growers (not all) agree the flower stalk and immature umbel should be removed just above the top leaf in order to focus the plant's energy on the bulb. If not removed, the energy required to produce the stalk and mature the bulbils may well reduce bulb size significantly. Most vegetables produce seed at the expense of the edible portion of the plant; thus, growers can rarely produce both a food crop and a seed crop. Topsetting garlics are more forgiving than most vegetables, but the same general rule applies.

On the other hand, the necessity of stalk removal is not universally agreed upon. We know a few good growers who never remove the stalks, yet consistently have high yields and high quality. Soil and climate appear to be decisive factors. The more fertile the soil and the more vigorous the plants, the less important it may be to "pop tops." The specific garlic strain is also a factor. Certain strains seem to produce large bulbs in good soil whether tops are popped or not. Others always produce very small bulbs, regardless of soil, when tops are left on.

In our own experiments with Spanish Roja (a Rocambole), we've measured average decreases in bulb size of about one-quarter inch for every additional week that tops are left intact after the coil in the flower stalk is first formed. But, even that measurement is relative. In very fertile soil, it may mean harvesting 2.25 inch bulbs instead of 2.5 inch bulbs—both quite large. In poor soil, it may mean average 1.5 inch bulbs instead of 2 inch bulbs—a decided decrease in total harvest weight and value.

We've also determined that non-Rocambole type ophio garlics suffer more loss in bulb size than do Rocamboles in general. That's because they produce taller flower stalks and spend a longer period of time producing and maturing bulbils than do Rocamboles. We haven't yet tested enough non-Rocamboles to be sure this trait is universal. Growers will have to decide for themselves whether popping tops is a benefit. We generally recommend it for market garlic but we know individual experiences will vary.

A far touchier subject is the question of **when** to pop tops. Common sense suggests "the earlier the better." Every day that the flower stalk is allowed to grow, energy is being used that could have been directed to the bulb instead. But the effects of "too early" and "too late" (versus "just the right time") are widely debated even among very experienced growers.

When we first started growing garlic, we visited the Christopher Ranch in Gilroy, California, where we received a lot of good advice from an old Japanese gentleman. While admitting (rather enviously) that topsetting garlics didn't perform well in California, he seemed extremely knowledgeable.

"The flower stalks should be removed from these garlics," he stated, "to help the garlic make stronger sheaths so it will store longer."

"When?" we asked.

"The sooner, the better," he replied matter-of-factly, "but not before the flower stalks curl; otherwise, the spears may try to grow back again."

The first ten years I grew ophio garlic, I popped the tops as soon as the coil was fully developed. So did all the other growers I knew. I don't know of anyone even experimenting with earlier removal, though I did ask several other old-timers about it. All of them gave answers based on instinct rather than experience. They believed early removal of stalks before the coil was formed might shock the plant too much and cause any one of several adverse reactions, such as secondary sprouting of cloves, or formation of side cloves off the main bulb. (Let me stress again that I've never experimented with early stalk removal myself.)

My views on flower stalk removal did change in the late 1980s. Nearly all the garlic growers in my county began to notice their Spanish Roja crops (the most popular local ophio garlic, by far) weren't storing as long as they used to. My own crop stored so poorly in 1986 and 1987 that I ended up composting a large portion of the crop both years. Bulbs were softening and dehydrating so severely by mid-September that we didn't finish cleaning and grading the crop in 1987.

I called numerous other growers and found most of them having the same experience. None of them could explain the cause of the problem, but nearly one-third announced they would not replant Spanish Roja in 1988 because high storage losses were making the cultigen unprofitable. I decided it was time to experiment in earnest.

In 1987, I left the flower stalks on one full bed of Spanish Roja, then harvested the plants and cured them with flower stalks and umbels intact. The plants were left hanging in the warehouse all winter. Once a month I felt the bulbs and squeezed them, then removed one bunch of ten plants, cleaned and bagged them. The main crop was seriously dehydrated by October 1st, but the plants with flower stalks intact remained hard as a rock all winter; in fact, they stored longer than any Roja I'd ever grown.

Curiously enough, my next door neighbor was also experimenting—quite unintentionally. His 1985 and 1986 crops stored more poorly than most other local growers because penicillium decay became a serious problem. He wanted to replace all his planting stock and start fresh, but financial difficulties ruled out that option. In desperation, he decided to let his 1987 crop fully mature the bulbils. He reasoned that blue-green molds should not be transmitted on bulbils. The process of sizing the bulbils up to market-sized bulbs would take at least two to three years, but in the end it should free him of penicillium decay.

My neighbors whole crop experiment in 1987 was part of the reason I'd left the flower stalks on one bed of garlic in 1987. Not surprisingly, his garlic stored hard as a rock all winter, the same as my experimental batch. Yet, I was still hesitant. After all, this went against ten years of tradition that had been passed on to us by experts. I actually considered it quite risky to involve half my 1988 crop in another experiment.

Yet, the evidence seemed overwhelming. Our storage problem could not have been caused by storage conditions, by bacteria or disease, nor by harvesting too early because plants from the same field stored all winter after receiving the same exact treatment and storage—except their flower stalks were never broken off. Nevertheless, I was cautiously optimistic. What if the long storage was a weird fluke of nature that couldn't be repeated? Some bulb size had definitely been sacrificed in my experiment. I didn't want to risk the whole crop and end up with the same wide variation in bulb sizes. A few of the experimental bulbs were tiny and a few were large, but the majority were intermediate in size (1.5 to 2 inch) and clearly small enough that my profitability would be affected.

As harvest approached in 1988, I was very excited, and very nervous as well about the possibility of decreased bulb size on half my crop if I waited too long to pop tops. I reasoned that stalk removal about seven to ten days after the coil formed should present an acceptable compromise—a little reduction in size but a lot better storage. The problem was that I couldn't be sure until I'd actually done it. My farming experience had taught me years earlier that what seemed logical in my brain was not always bio-logical to plants.

Flower stalks on the main crop coiled. We removed them right on schedule. I checked the remaining plants at least every other day thereafter, searching for a clue as to when I should stop delaying and pop the rest of the tops. Within about one week, the remaining flower stalks began to lose their curl and stand up straight, an event I knew should occur—but I hadn't been mentally prepared for the sight of an entire field of stalks rising four to five feet in the air like dancing serpents. It was impressive, and nerve wracking.

When about half the remaining plants had lost the coil in their flower stalk, I went out one evening to begin popping tops and was surprised to find the stalks had turned quite woody. I couldn't snap them off with a quick flick of the wrist and soon resorted to cutting them with a sharp knife. The task took longer than normal, so I had plenty of time to reflect.

Why had the flower stalks turned woody? Because the plant was maturing? Could they be maturing any differently than the stalkless plants across the field where I now expected harvest to begin within about one week? Not outwardly. But where does all the moisture in the succulent flower stalk disappear to when the stalk turns woody? What message must be sent to the bulb when the plant began hardening its stalk?

The term "hardening" immediately caught my attention. I straightened up slowly (my aching back wouldn't let me stand up rapidly) and stared at the tall, straight flower stalks ahead of me. "Hardening off," I said aloud to myself, and then repeated the words several times out loud. A smile began to form. What if the processes of "hardening off" and "maturation" were not the same? Garlic always matures even when harvested a month early. It matures by forming clove skins around the cloves as it dries down. Maybe the process of hardening off was different.

Over the course of the next few days, I reasoned that hormones must be somehow involved here. The woody flower stalks weren't simply drying down, they were standing up tall. The process must require energy. Hormones had to be telling the plant what to do. Perhaps the standing of the stalks was also related to the hardening off of the bulbs. Yet the plants weren't drying down yet.

If hardening off was a natural process linked with the loss of the stalk curl and the woodification of the stalks, then what message would early flower stalk removal send to the bulbs? Perhaps a distress signal that said "Grow more vigorously (i.e. don't dry down or harden off yet), we've lost our bulbils and our survival now depends on the cloves." Such a surge of growth must require a very different kind of hormones than a hardening off process.

I still can't explain the exact bio-chemical process, let alone the specific changes that might be initiated by early flower stalk removal. I do know the experimental half of the 1988 crop stored much longer than the portion whose stalks were broken off as soon as they coiled. In 1989 and 1990 we removed all stalks only after they turned woody and lost their coils. If we could still snap them easily with our fingers, then we waited. When the flower stalks had to be cut with a knife, we forged ahead.

I'm fairly convinced now (four years after our first experiments) that our ophio garlics store longer (stay in a period of rest, or dormancy, longer) specifically because the bulb and stalk are allowed to harden off before the stalks are removed. In 1990, flower stalk removal occurred only three days prior to the start of harvest. Our bulbs were the same large size we've grown accustomed to, so I'm convinced late stalk removal doesn't necessarily mean reduced bulb size.

However, our reports of better storage for ophio garlics because of late stalk removal also generated some controversy. There are still a lot of growers nationwide who dispute our claim, some quite emotionally as if we were trying to ruin the small farm garlic industry in America. So far, the letters and phone calls run about 50-50 for and against late flower stalk removal. We even continue to get a few calls from surprised growers who've never removed flower stalks and just don't understand what all the fuss is about.

Definite conclusion: there is none. Each grower will have to experiment and derive his or her own conclusion. I *can* speculate, however, that many of the growers who complain about late flower stalk removal causing small bulbs are either at much higher elevations or more northern latitudes than we are. Many also grow garlic in generally poorer soils with less organic matter. I suspect our tendency to experience one hundred degree Fahrenheit temperatures earlier in the season and over a longer portion of the growing season than growers at higher elevations is a definite factor. I suspect the combination of severe heat and early flower stalk removal forces early maturity and earlier drying down of the plant. I think the result may be garlic that's forced to mature so rapidly it doesn't have time to harden off. In a typical year, that may result in bulbs with lower soluble solids and thinner clove skins—exactly the kind of bulb one would expect to dehydrate and soften rather than store a long time.

Not all growers face the same combinations of weather we do. Growers only forty miles away, but at two thousand feet higher elevation, typically harvest four to five weeks later than we do. I've collected bulb samples and found them to store extremely well despite early flower stalk removal. So, I can't give advice, only my suspicions that growers with poor to moderate soils need to remove flower stalks earlier than growers with highly fertile soils and intense pre-harvest temperatures. If topsetters store poorly for you, try letting the flower stalks turn woody before cutting them off.

Pre-Harvest Tips

The moisture needs of garlic decrease during the final month before harvest. Plant roots must be able to find enough moisture to sustain the process of bulbing, hardening off, bulbil production, etc., but not as much as they needed when the plant was growing green succulent leaves. Wet topsoils are highly conducive to most fungi, and this becomes especially critical as the bulbs are maturing. The dry down of the first few leaves signifies that the outer bulb wrappers beneath the soil are on the verge of decay which can attract all sorts of soil microorganisms—both desirable and undesirable. Ideally, moisture is maintained in the root zone without the topsoil and bulbs being very wet.

On the other hand, cutting the water off altogether can force early maturity and loss of bulb size. The question of when to stop irrigating is always difficult for garlic growers who irrigate. Most of them apply the final irrigation two to three weeks before actual harvest. Growers without irrigation can only pray that the weather favors a good harvest.

We commonly brush the topsoil away from ten or twelve random plants in the field in order to expose the bulbs for inspection. We check to see if the soil seems too wet or dry, and to see how developed the bulbs are. If the garlic is still mulched and the mulch is too wet, we may decide to remove all the mulch, especially if there is the threat of rain. Are bulbs well sized? Is there enough plant vigor and soil moisture to allow the bulbs time to finish swelling? What condition are the bulb wrappers in? Decay and breakdown of outer bulb wrappers indicate maturity is at hand or even past.

Excess soil moisture and high nutrient levels (especially nitrogen) can be disastrous in combination with overmature bulbs. The result may be one of two extremes— plants that stay green and refuse to stop growing despite large, well developed bulbs, or plants that keep growing green leaves while refusing to develop bulbs at all.

In general, the condition of the plant above ground should be in harmony with the parts below ground. If leaf drydown is well advanced while stem swelling (i.e. bulbing) is just beginning, then something is wrong. More than likely the soil is too dry. Plants should be redirecting some of their nutrients and energy from the top of the plant down into the bulb so that the bulb swells as the leaves **start** to dry down. Bulbs should be well-sized by the time about 25% of the plant leaves are brown.

Many growers fall behind on weeding during the final month or two of the season. It may require too much time for a complete weeding, but weeds can still use up needed soil moisture and contribute to early drydown. Nutrient competition is seldom critical at this stage, but moisture loss may be, so don't stop weeding entirely just because harvest is only four or five weeks away.

More importantly, rank weed growth may contribute to

high moisture levels at ground level. Sunlight and good air circulation are essential to the gradual drying of the soil and the hardening off of the plant. Molds may flourish in damp rank weeds where sunlight is limited and humidity high.

Many growers are fooled by failing to realize that certain weeds germinate late in the season at high soil temperatures and then grow very rapidly. Good early season weeding can be to no avail if the hot weather weeds are allowed to overwhelm the garlic in the month before harvest. In my region, hot weather weeds include various knotweeds, morning glory, clovers, mallow, pigweed, and a host of others. Most of them are broad-leaved, sunloving plants that mature and produce seed very rapidly. Even if they don't directly interfere with garlic development or maturation, they may make harvest physically miserable in addition to scattering seven more years worth of weed seeds into the soil.

PART III

Harvest to Market

Harvest and Curing

It serves little purpose to grow good garlic if the plants can't be properly harvested and cured. Growers have to decide the optimum time to harvest, and that will vary year to year. Both time of harvest and the curing environment are important if you expect the garlic to store well. While most gardeners can windrow or hang plants on a porch to cure, farmers need to plan ahead and be prepared for inclement weather. Growers in humid climates often have to take extra precautions to prevent molding.

When to Harvest

I harvest garlic based on the number of **green** plant leaves remaining—not the number of brown or dead leaves. Most garden-type reference books tell you to harvest garlic after tops have turned brown and fallen over. Some even suggest you should break the tops over if they aren't dying back fast enough. My advice is, don't take their advice, especially regarding ophio garlics. The generic garden books are probably referring to Artichoke garlics (softneck) which can, admittedly, be left in the ground to dry down fairly thoroughly in some years, but such plants are harder to harvest (they usually have to be dug out so that tops don't pull off) and are more susceptible to storage molds.

If garlic plants are allowed to turn completely brown before harvest then bulbs are overmature and sometimes split open like a blossoming flower, a condition that invites decay of the outer bulb wrappers. The initiation of decay is an invitation to a multitude of soil micro-organisms, including various fungi (i.e. molds). If soils are not too wet, the decay is liable to be minimal and easily removed when the bulbs are cleaned, but it's a somewhat risky proposition. As soon as bulbs begin to split open, the bulb wrappers at the neck of the bulb tend to split apart so that dirt and moisture can fall inside the bulb where they are trapped. It doesn't take much moisture to encourage the growth of molds because the soil particles are sure to contain fungal spores. Overnight dew or a slight rainfall, even poor air circulation during the curing process, might be enough to start the mold growing, and mold inside the bulb can't be removed during the cleaning process. These bulbs are simply harder to store regardless of storage conditions.

There is a difference in the optimum harvest times for the different varieties of garlic. Artichoke garlics (subspecies *sativum*, or softneck) are harvested first at most locations, generally a few days to one week ahead of topsetting ophio garlics. Silverskin garlics (also subspecies *sativum*) are harvested last at our location.

As already mentioned, the time of harvest for Artichoke garlics is less critical than for ophio garlics. Artichoke bulbs aren't nearly as likely to split open in the ground unless soils are very wet. They do, however, lose bulb wrappers as they become overmature. This tends to leave the outer layer of cloves exposed. The bulbs are then rough looking, and the exposed cloves are more susceptible to bruising; in fact, they tend to break off from the bulb during shipping and handling. Loose cloves translate into losses for grocery stores. The idea, then, is to harvest Artichoke garlics with a full complement of bulb wrappers.

We harvest Artichoke bulbs when they still have at least five green leaves. If you have a large crop that will require more than a few days to harvest, I suggest starting when plants still have an average of six green leaves. Remember that plants with green leaves require very good curing conditions. Air circulation is essential in order to prevent molds from growing on slowly drying stems and leaves that were still green when pulled from the ground. If curing conditions are less than optimal, you may want to let the plants dry down more in the ground before harvest.

We use the number of green leaves as the key factor determining time of harvest because each green leaf represents a good solid bulb wrapper. Brown or dead leaves represent bulb wrappers either non-existent (i.e. already decayed) or in early stages of decay. In other words, brown leaves above ground usually indicate bulb wrappers that will be lost as the garlic is harvested, cured, and cleaned.

We like an absolute minimum of three good bulb wrappers after the bulbs are cleaned and ready for shipment. Four or five wrappers is even better. We plan on losing at least one wrapper during harvest, and one to two additional wrappers when we clean and grade the bulbs. That's a net loss of two to three leaves. If bulbs are handled several more times (repackaged, jostled a lot during shipment, displayed on store shelves, and then handled by the customer as well) they'll probably lose at least one more wrapper—which totals a net loss of three to four wrappers by the time the bulb comes to rest in someone's kitchen.

Six green leaves at harvest, minus three to four during cleaning and handling, equals two to three remaining wrappers to protect the garlic for the consumer. By contrast, four green leaves at harvest means zero to one remaining wrappers for the consumer. The life of the bulbs may be considerably shortened with only zero to one bulb wrappers. Individual cloves are then more susceptible to bruising and puncture, moisture loss, and dehydration. Artichoke garlics are generally more immune to moisture loss than ophio garlics, but bulb wrappers are present to protect the cloves from the surrounding environment (air, light, heat, etc). Fewer bulb wrappers means less protection.

Ophio garlics are more difficult to manage than Artichokes because leaves and bulb wrappers are more susceptible to decay if left in the soil too long. Cloves are more likely to have broken or split clove skins inside the bulb wrappers, so the cloves need more protection. Overmature bulbs start to split open in the ground much faster than do Artichoke garlics.

We harvest topsetters when an average of six green

leaves remain. Leaves start to brown at the tips, and leaves at the bottom of the plant brown first. We typically check twenty plants each in several sections of the field. As soon as the sixth green leaf is starting to turn brown at the tip on fifty percent of the crop, we begin harvest. We hope to complete harvest within three days, but we seldom do. Some growers prefer to use the percentage of total green remaining because the total number of plant leaves varies from year to year. They harvest when plants are about 40% browned and 60% green. Overmature ophio garlics are nearly impossible to store more than a few months. We think it's better to harvest a little early than a little late.

Silverskins are last. We used to feel that they could stand more drying before harvest than Artichoke garlics and topsetters, but the last few years have convinced me to start earlier—again, when about six plant leaves are still green. The quality of the bulb wrappers after curing seems much better than when we harvest at a three to four green leaf stage.

We're going to start experimenting with refractometers in 1991. It seems quite possible that peak maturity and optimum harvest might arrive earlier or later some years rather than correlating exactly with leaf dry down. "Maturity" isn't always easy to judge; indeed, it's a hard term for some folks to understand at all. It's not a precise point on a line so much as a brief four-dimensional window. The chief factor determining maturity is the percentage of soluble solids that may be measured by refractometers. Secondary factors are the thickness, texture, and moisture content of bulb wrappers and clove skins, but skins tend to form and harden even when garlic is harvested well ahead of true maturity. All the factors progress from stages of immaturity to eventual stages of overmaturity, but not at the same rates. Optimum maturity is when all the factors are as close as possible to the so-called window. If any one factor goes too far beyond the window into some degree of overmaturity, storage and marketability will be shortened.

Perhaps an apple analogy can be more easily understood. Undermature apples are still very starchy and not very sweet. The underside of the skin is still greenish in color, and, on partially red apples, the background color is still greenish rather than yellowish. These apples are bland tasting unless stored a long time.

Overmature apples are very sweet (the starches have been converted to sugars, and the sugar is beginning to break down (natural sugars are fairly unstable compared to starches). The apple loses crispness as starch turns to sugar. In technical terms, an overmature (or "dead ripe") apple is already in the early stages of decay. It may taste good, but it won't store very long before turning mushy. In short, there's a thin line between a dead ripe apple and a rotten apple.

Ripe apples (initial maturity) have just the right combination of sweetness, crispness and color. They will store reasonably well because decay (or overmaturity) has not yet begun. The cooler the temperature, the slower the eventual decay.

The stages of garlic maturation are less pronounced than for apples, but the process is essentially the same. Immature garlic lacks character and flavor, although average consumers will never notice the subtle difference. Overmature bulbs won't store very long before serious deterioration begins. Unlike an apple, a "dead ripe" garlic bulb can be easily recognized from a great distance because of the strong sulphurous gases it emits. When those gases combine with the bacterial decay that readily attacks overmature garlic flesh, well...it stinks to high heaven.

Overmature Artichoke garlics store fairly well compared to ophio garlics if the humidity isn't too high, but they still may not market well because of their rough appearance. All is not necessarily lost, however. Bulbs intended as planting stock are commonly left in the ground longer than table stock because they don't have to store and because overmature bulbs are easier to pop apart for planting. Planting stock doesn't need thick beautiful bulb wrappers. Growers, thus, have two possible markets for slightly overmature bulbs: table stock if the garlic will be sold and consumed fairly rapidly—about two months for ophio garlic and three to four months for sativums—or planting stock if the bulbs came from vigorous healthy plants.

How to Harvest ————————————————

The onset of overmaturity may be quite rapid in hot weather. Garlic harvest is basically one of those tasks that doesn't wait around until a convenient time. In our region it also usually corresponds with the hottest week of the year. Soil temperatures may reach 120 degrees Fahrenheit on the surface when air temperatures approach 100 degrees Fahrenheit in mid-afternoon. These temperatures can actually cook the flesh inside the clove skins if freshly pulled plants are left in direct sunlight more than a few minutes at a time. The flesh of cooked garlic (or "sunburned" garlic) turns a translucent yellow and spoils very quickly.

Our routine involves pulling the plants by hand, rubbing the dirt from the roots, and bundling the plants ten at a time with a six foot length of baler twine. "Pullers" lay the bundles behind them as they work down the bed, but they make sure that "stackers" are never more than a few bundles behind. Stackers place the garlic upright in a truck with a canopy or temporary shield so that plants are not in direct sunlight. When the truck is full, the whole crew migrates to the warehouse. The idea is to get the garlic into the warehouse as fast as possible. After all, soil temperatures a few inches beneath the surface are usually sixty to seventy degrees Fahrenheit while the air temperature is at least eighty to ninety degrees Fahrenheit. We stop harvesting late in the morning when air temperatures reach about ninety degrees Fahrenheit, and start again in the evening. The sudden shock and rapid drying when bulbs leave the protection of the soil can affect the quality of the garlic. We want the bulbs to experience moderate temperature and humidity changes if possible.

Our warehouse rarely rises above seventy-five degrees Fahrenheit even on very hot days. We would like the garlic to go from soil to warehouse very quickly so that curing proceeds at approximately the same temperatures that bulbs would have experienced had they continued to cure in the ground.

Many growers can't hand pull plants the way we can in rich fluffy soil. Alternatives include the hard and tried shovel or potato fork method (loosening the soil under each bulb, one at a time), or pulling a tool bar beneath the rows or beds to loosen the soil and cut the plant roots. As with mechanized cultivation, tractor drawn tool bars may damage a few bulbs. We've seen modified potato diggers uproot garlic, separate bulbs from dirt, and plop the plants on top of the ground where they're easily retrieved. However, it takes some skill to create a machine that doesn't bruise the bulbs or tangle the plant leaves in the rollers. In semi-arid climates, it's also critical that the harvester not get too far ahead of the laborers so the plants don't lie in the sun too long.

The potential damage caused by sudden direct sunlight for periods of only ten to twenty minutes should not be underestimated. It's the chief reason we don't follow the advice of most reference books about windrowing the plants after harvest. Windrowing involves laying the pulled plants so they cover the bulbs of the previous row with plant leaves. Large commercial growers commonly windrow garlic in this manner for two to three days as the initial step in the curing process. We've tried it and experienced very poor results (as have many other growers). No wonder when you think about it. The purpose of windrowing is to dry the leaves and bulbs. If leaves are expected to shrivel in one hundred degree heat, how can they also be expected to cover and protect the bulbs? The answer, I suppose, is that there's a real art to windrowing garlic. We strongly recommend against windrowing for small scale growers who want to produce top quality market garlic.

There is another reason we don't like windrowing, and it's liable to generate some controversy. We believe there is a difference between the "curing" of garlic and the "rapid drying" of garlic. Perhaps it's a subtle point, but my instincts tell me that any sudden extreme change in environment may shock the garlic and damage its integrity. Maybe it's because I think of harvested garlic plants as *live* food. Or maybe it's my limited experience collecting herbs and dried flowers where I was taught that the time of day of harvest, the rate of cure, and the intensity of the heat all have a direct effect on the chemical composition, potency, and appearance of the final dried product.

Right or wrong, we cure garlic somewhat slowly in a warehouse with very little temperature or humidity fluctuation. Warehouse temperatures normally stay between sixty-five to seventy-five degrees Fahrenheit in July and August (usually staying within two or three degrees of the mean daily average outdoor temperature) rather than varying between forty degrees at night and ninety degrees or more at midday. I believe garlic cures better at a more constant temperature than when it experiences daily extremes. Temperature extremes cause rapid expansion and contraction of cell walls. They also affect the internal chemistry of cloves.

There is no real mystery in all this talk of temperature ranges during the curing process. Place a soil thermometer two to three inches below the surface and see how much the temperature varies over a typical twenty four hour period in July. If it varies more than ten degrees, you probably have a faulty thermometer. This is where garlic cures in nature—in the soil where it is well buffered from extreme temperature and humidity changes between day and night. I'd like to mimic the natural process as closely as possible.

That does not mean growers should panic because they don't have warehouses with temperature controls. The majority of small growers feel fortunate to find an old barn or a shed, and they've grown and cured good garlic for years under those less than ideal conditions. The most important considerations are simply good air circulation and protection from direct sun. Additional controls aren't essential unless you live in a constantly wet, humid environment where garlic rots before it has a chance to cure.

Another harvesting debate involves the addition of bulb washing, and/or top and root trimming to the actual harvest process. I'll be honest. I think these are simple shortcuts, and shorcuts can get you into trouble. If I'm going from point A to point B in a car, I sometimes take a shortcut, but there are no shorcuts to top quality gourmet garlic.

I go to a lot of trouble to decrease soil moisture before harvest. I don't want to pull wet bulbs from the soil because that condition invites mold and decay as well as stained skins and tough-to-clean skins. Why then would I wash bulbs immediately after harvest? I consider it another question of integrity, and I think the integrity of the carefully matured bulbs is greatly compromised when bulbs are suddenly and rudely plunged into bathwater. I know that some people still do it (primarily because the washed bulbs look perfectly clean and shiny), but I can't recommend the practise. In fact, I've seen washed bulbs mold in at least one instance, and develop badly wrinkled bulb wrappers in another. Both disasters could have been avoided by taking the long route instead of the shortcut.

The second most common reason for washing bulbs is not that washed bulbs look so clean, but that unwashed bulbs are nearly impossible to clean. I know that certain soils simply won't rub off of cured bulbs, but soil texture is the key in the long run—not bathwater. Tight soils with very little organic matter dry hard and fast, especially if they contain high proportions of silt and clay. Light soils with lots of humus have texture, and they clean up fairly easily. Better to lighten up the soil with a good serious soil enhancement program.

My feelings about root clipping and removal of leaves and stems in the field immediately after harvest are similar, though the actions are not as distasteful as the thought of washed garlic. Obviously, bulbs free of roots and tops are lighter, and they take up less space. By trimming roots and tops in the field, growers can kill two birds with one stone, but I suspect the bulbs cure better with roots and tops intact. I trust my instincts on this one even though I know at least half a dozen growers who disagree with me (and grow good garlic to boot).

My instinct about the "integrity" of garlic bulbs is not completely unfounded. For example, Egyptian researchers in an extensive series of experiments found that disease incidence in stored garlic was reduced nearly two-thirds by curing the bulbs before cutting off the necks.*

Most growers will choose their own medicine. We try to start the curing process in the soil, then move the plants from the soil to the warehouse as quickly as possible and with as little change in temperature, humidity, and plant character as possible. The plants then take two to four weeks to cure, depending on the weather. We don't begin to trim, clean, and grade the bulbs until curing is complete enough that the outer bulb wrappers are dry and easily removed.

Some growers begin cleaning and grading the crop as soon after harvest as possible. Usually it's because they're anxious to sell the crop on the early market and have money in their pockets. There's nothing terribly wrong with early marketing of partially cured garlic (sometimes called "green garlic"), as long as the buyer knows what is being bought. After all, partially cured bulbs weigh between 10% and 25% more than cured garlic. Green garlic also requires packaging in smaller units (e.g. twenty pound packs), and it will need better than normal ventilation to prevent it from heating up, sweating, and molding. With proper packaging and handling the consumer can still take home great tasting fresh garlic. But green garlic is also much harder to clean. Growers have to put in some extra effort in order to make the bulbs look presentable for the marketplace.

One final note about curing. Growers in humid climates have to take extra precautions. Indoor curing with good ventilation and at least some control over humidity are highly desirable. If air is not dry enough to even dry the plant roots after harvest, I'd make an exception and trim the roots as soon as possible (not the tops, however). Garlic roots have an amazing capacity to collect moisture out of thin air.

During curing, wet tops can prevent the bulb itself from drying. If mold begins forming on the necks then there's a good chance it will also form inside the bulbs on the cloves. Fans may be required to force air through the plants, and a dry heat source may be necessary to lower the humidity in some climates. These are serious considerations for humid climate garlic growers. One of the ultimate frustrations is to spend nine months planting, grow-

*Abstract 2422, *Horticultural Abstracts*, 60(4), April 1990, p. 280.

ing, and harvesting a beautiful crop only to watch it rot before it can be cleaned and marketed—and I've seen it happen in the maritime northwest more times than I care to remember.

Cleaning, Grading, & Packaging

I'm always shocked to find good farmers who consistently grow high quality food crops and then send them to market poorly cleaned, poorly graded, and shabbily packaged. We live in a consumer society where all the hard work on the farm is wasted if the final product isn't appealing to the customer and easy to handle and identify by the produce people and truckers.

Cleaning, grading, and packaging of gourmet, fresh market garlic require alert people with sharp eyes and quick hands. Quality is almost always more important to small-scale growers than quantity, so "fast" is not synonymous with efficient; in fact, efficiency is misguided if high quality is not the result.

All our cleaning, grading and packaging is done by hand, one bulb at a time. It seems a completely anachronistic process to graduates of agribusiness universities and schools of agricultural engineering, but we're really producing a handcrafted work of art more than a mass food commodity. By and large, our customers do notice the extra care and quality.

Cleaning —————————————————

We start by clipping the necks. Both topsetters (with woody stems) and subspecies *sativum* (with soft necks) can be clipped with scissors, but topsetters require sharp, heavy-duty scissors. Dull tools may leave a sharp point or jagged edge on topsetters if the woody stems break or tear rather than cutting cleanly. Sharp edges will certainly puncture other bulbs when packaged and shipped.

A number of growers actually chop the garlic necks

(especially of ophio garlics) with a sharp hatchet or machete and find it quicker and more rhythmical than scissors. I prefer this method as long as the "choppers" have insured fingers. All kidding aside, choppers need no more than a moderately sharp blow from a short height if they're wielding a sharp tool. I've never heard of anyone injured using this method, but wielders of sharp scissors cut their fingers and hands quite commonly. I suspect that people naturally tend to be more careful with hatchets and machetes than with scissors.

Actually, the greatest problems with hatchets and machetes is the potential to bruise the bulb. Plants can't simply be laid on a flat surface; rather, the bulb has to hang over the edge of a good solid cutting board in such a position that cloves aren't bruised and bulb wrappers aren't split or cracked from the force of the blow.

We leave about one-half inch of neck on ophio garlics and less on sativums. The international garlic standards of the European Economic Community state that stems of dried garlic shall not exceed three centimeters, but we know from experience that one-quarter to one-half inch stems make convenient handles for anyone trying to pry loose a clove. They also insure that bulb wrappers remain intact at the top of the bulb. If necks are cut too short, the tops of the cloves are readily exposed to the outside environment, including small insects and disease organisms.

Next, roots are trimmed to the same length (one-quarter to one-half inch). This is partly to prevent roots from collecting moisture, but mostly to impart a neat and trimmed look to the bulb. Of course, dried dirt must also be rubbed loose from the remaining tuft. We know many growers who cut the roots flush with the bulb (the European standard), but we think the garlic looks less natural. We've had old-timers tell us that bulbs store better with a tuft of roots remaining, but I suspect the opposite may actually be true. Preferences vary, not only between nations and cultures, but between specific produce buyers and consumers.

Final bulb cleaning involves the bulb wrappers and probably entails some art as well as skill. The idea is to remove as few bulb wrappers as possible while ending up with an undamaged bulb that has both clean and unbroken outer wrappers. Only one wrapper need be removed from most bulbs to accomplish this, but inexperienced cleaners may quickly find themselves staring at exposed cloves if they employ the wrong techniques. It takes just the right touch to coax a single skin away with a downward and outward motion of the thumb from top to bottom. Too much pressure may break through all the wrappers near the neck. A few bulbs may need two or three wrappers removed before a clean, unbroken one is found, but these should constitute a definite minority if bulbs are grown in good soil and well cured before cleaning.

It's extremely common for wrappers to adhere tightly to the bulb on the bottom side near the roots. Here we employ a medium-bristled toothbrush. Most growers will want to remove just enough obvious dirt that the bulb can be handled without any loose clumps falling free. In other words, they don't mind if a thin layer of dried dirt refuses to come off. We go one step further and require that our bulbs also look clean no matter what the viewing angle.

Most bulbs "clean up" with a few quick strokes of the brush. Here again, some skill is required. The bristles should not be angled into the bulb; rather, they should point in a downward direction parallel with the bulb surface. The bristles of the brush are supposed to slip under the edges of broken wrappers—wrappers are lifted off rather than brushed off. Too much vigor or too much of an angle into the bulb and the remaining wrappers will be penetrated.

We sell gourmet garlic. You may choose a less perfect goal, depending on your intended market. Most customers don't seem to demand spotless bulbs, but they do seem to remember them and often exclaim over them. "How did you get these bulbs so clean and beautiful?" Those words are music to my ears.

Grading

Cleaners have other responsibilities, too. When they first pick up a bulb, a light squeeze should tell them whether the bulb is dehydrating. We cull out soft bulbs since they'll only get softer while waiting to get to market. Damaged and diseased bulbs also get culled. Most cull bulbs tend to have a single bad clove, so the cleaners should be constantly aware of the texture of the bulb as it is turned round in their fingers.

Our goal is to cull all bulbs with obvious damage, too few bulb wrappers, noticeable dehydration, damaged roots, stained skins, exposed clove flesh, or abnormal bulb shape (such as flat-sided bulbs). We want market bulbs to look uniform in shape, quality, and size.

Most of the growers we know size their bulbs in one-half inch increments, and they measure bulbs from side to side at the widest point. Some use ring sizers, but most hold the bulb by the stem and pass it between a v-shaped pattern of nails in a board until the bulb rests against two nails it can't fit between. We've sized this way for years and never found anything faster and more accurate. Obviously, it's important not to bang the bulbs against the nails. Likewise, sized bulbs can't simply be dropped in a bag or thrown into a box. Garlic bruises far more readily than most people realize. If we drop a bulb on the table or floor, it gets culled.

While one-half inch grades seem to be the unofficial standard accepted and used by most small scale producers of fresh market garlic in the western United States, we discovered early on that a potential problem existed, especially when garlic from two different growers was placed side by side. It wasn't uncommon for most of one batch to consist of bulbs just under two inches in diameter while most of the second batch consisted of bulbs just over 1.5 inches. The two batches were the same size-grade, but one looked obviously smaller. We decided that one-half inch grades weren't uniform enough. Today we use one-quarter inch increments even though we may sell two adjacent grades under the same one-half inch size name to buyers who prefer the standard grades. Our garlic ends up looking more uniform when displayed to the customer.

The three most popular size grades for small garlic growers in the western U.S. are Large (1.5 to 2 inches), Extra Large (2 to 2.5 inches), and Premium (2.5 inches minimum). Filaree Farm size grades are Medium (1.5 to 1.75 inches), Large (1.75 to 2 inches), Extra Large (2 to 2.25 inches), Jumbo (2.25 to 2.5 inches), and Premium (2.5 inches minimum). We primarily market ophio garlics, but sativum bulbs are sometimes large enough that we could create a "Colossal" size for 3 inch minimum bulbs.

We also started measuring bulb diameter at the narrowest rather than the widest point. The difference may seem negligible, but it's not. We give the buyer the benefit of the doubt. If the garlic bulb is borderline in size and could fall into either size-grade, we always downgrade it. The result is that our garlic looks (and really is) a little bigger than the same size-grade garlic from other growers.

In short, from start to finish, we go the extra mile so customers take note of our garlic. Ideally, we want buyers and consumers to have a memorable experience when they open our boxes—something that registers in their brain (and taste buds) as uncommon and above the ordinary. It requires extra work at the farm, but it pays dividends once a reputation for top quality is established.

The United States standards for commercial garlic are available from the Fruit and Vegetable Division, Agricultural Marketing Service, Washington, D.C. 20250. In general, they're far less strict than we are at Filaree Farm. They provide for only one grade, "U.S. #1," which must consist of garlic of similar varietal characteristics (e.g. of the same color) which is well cured; mature; compact with cloves well filled and fairly plump (i.e. not shrivelled); free from mold, decay, shattered cloves; and free from damage caused by dirt, staining, sunscald, cuts, sprouts, tops, roots, disease, insects, or mechanical means. Each bulb shall be fairly well enclosed in its outer sheath and, unless otherwise specified, shall have a minimum diameter of not less than 1.5 inches. "Mature and well cured" is defined as having reached that stage of development at which the garlic is firm and sufficiently dried so as not to be soft and spongy. "Compact" is defined to mean that cloves are not spreading but fit closely together practically the entire length of individual cloves. "Damage" is defined as any specific or other defect which materially detracts from the appearance, edibility, or marketing quality of the garlic.

The international standards of the European Economic Community (EEC) are somewhat less vague. Bulbs must be sound, firm, clean (especially free of dirt and residues), free of mold, sunscald, freeze damage, external sprouting, foreign smells or tastes, and unusual external moisture. The standards describe three quality grades— Extra, Class I, and Class II. "Extra" grade garlic must be whole, regular in shape, well cleaned, free of defects, etc. Class II grade garlic may have cracks on the outer bulb wrapper, healed cracks of mechanical origin, and slight bruising that is not liable to impair the garlic's keeping quality, such defects not to affect more than two cloves per bulb. Class II bulbs may also be irregular in shape and minus as many as three cloves. Class I bulbs must be whole, fairly regular in shape, and may have small cracks or slight overmaturity.

The international size standards are simple. Extra class garlic shall have a minimum bulb diameter of forty-five millimeters (about 1.75 inches). Class I and II bulbs shall have minimum diameters of at least 1.25 inches.

Packing

Cleaned, graded, dried garlic in the western United States is often shipped in forty pound netted onion bags. The bags are often "seconds" or reject bags that commercial onion growers ordered and never used because they were improperly stitched or mislabeled. Small growers turn the bags inside out. While the bags are convenient for short storage on the farm, they're not easy to ship and handle. Bulbs may be easily bruised when handlers toss the heavy bags around. Obviously, the bags don't stack very well. Garlic that isn't completely cured will sweat in the center of the pack. Twenty pound netted bags are sometimes available, but are only a slightly better choice.

Most growers now ship garlic in easy to handle, vented, cardboard boxes. There seems to be no standard size. We've seen twenty, thirty, forty, and fifty pound net boxes. The twenty pound cartons are our favorite here at Filaree Farm because they're more apt to be carefully picked up and set down than are bags. But the boxes are very poor containers for long term storage before shipment. We don't even trust the ventilated boxes for warehouse storage. Consequently, our garlic is bagged in twenty or forty pound netted bags for warehouse storage, then repacked in twenty pound cardboard cartons for shipment. The repackaging gives us an ideal chance to regrade the garlic after several months of warehouse storage. We want to be sure that only hard, firm bulbs are shipped to market.

We can reuse the netted onion bags for several years, but we replace them fairly regularly in order to decrease the possibility of spreading molds and diseases. About three years is the maximum. When other growers send us garlic we never reuse their netted bags. Under no circumstances do we ever use a netted onion bag that actually had commercial onions stored in them. We've never had a serious disease problem and we want to keep it that way.

When packing dried garlic bulbs we place a jiffy pad in the bottom of the box. Jiffy pads are made entirely of recycled paper that's shredded and then sandwiched between two smooth sheets. Apple packing sheds use them by the millions, and they cost us roughly a nickel each. We place a second pad on top of the garlic. Plastic is avoided as a packing material because it doesn't allow the garlic to breathe well.

When packing garlic, the largest bulbs are usually placed one at a time with stem and roots alternating. That keeps the bulbs from rolling around in transit. Small and medium size bulbs are normally loose packed. Damage to the bulbs in transit seems to be very minimal as long as the boxes are full. If the garlic doesn't quite reach the lid we add several more jiffy pads.

All shipped boxes have our farm label on one side of the box, the words "Washington Select Garlic" on the opposite side, and specific details about the contents and grower on one end. The labeling is critical. Shippers should be able to identify the contents, the net weight, and bulb size with no more than a quick glance. It's annoying to have to open the box to see what's inside, and even more annoying to have to weigh the box.

Farm labels are very important. Market tests have consistently proven that produce sells better when associated with a specific farm name. We think that geographic location is also helpful. Our small "Okanogan County" logo consists of an easily identified and remembered outline of Washington state with our county in black, and the words "Product of Washington State" around the outside. The label and the logo compliment each other well. Buyers have no trouble remembering the name because it's always associated with the geographic location on the logo (i.e. visual as well as name association).

Label design is worth spending some time and money on. Labels and logos don't work when they're complicated or wordy. The artwork should be graciously simple—not simplistic. The balance between words, artwork, and empty space is critical. The viewers eyes will immediately be drawn to only one spot on the label (unless they actually stop and study it). That one spot should usually be the farm name. The label must be designed so that the eyes are immediately drawn to the name. Everything else amounts to background or border—it compliments the name like a nice frame but doesn't actually draw the eyes away from the name.

Our boxes are two-piece Western Lugs, a standard size that's readily available in fruit producing areas in the western United States. You can pay to have boxes custom made, but it's expensive. The important thing is that all your boxes be the same size—single shipments of assorted recycled boxes are a nuisance to shippers and handlers. Uniformity is a key to marketing in our urban, standardized culture. Just remember that uniformity doesn't have to be the equivalent of standardized mediocrity

If cleaned garlic sits in our warehouse more than three weeks before shipment, we re-examine every bulb during packing. It's rare to find more than a few bad bulbs, but we'd rather no bad bulbs were shipped.

We try to arrange shipments for Monday or Tuesday so that garlic won't end up sitting in a warehouse over the weekend. Dried garlic bulbs aren't highly perishable produce, but time is still of the essence. The quicker the bulbs reach their destination, the longer their shelf life in the store or the consumers' kitchen.

A packing slip with our farm name and address and an itemized list of what's been shipped accompany every shipment. The packing slip isn't hidden inside one of the boxes—it's in plain sight in a standard "Packing Slip Envelope" that sticks well to any surface. Invoices are mailed separately.

When marking net weights on boxes, don't forget to allow for the weight of the box and packing materials. We usually weigh out 20.5 pounds of bulbs for boxes marked twenty pounds net. Once again, we give the customer the benefit of the doubt.

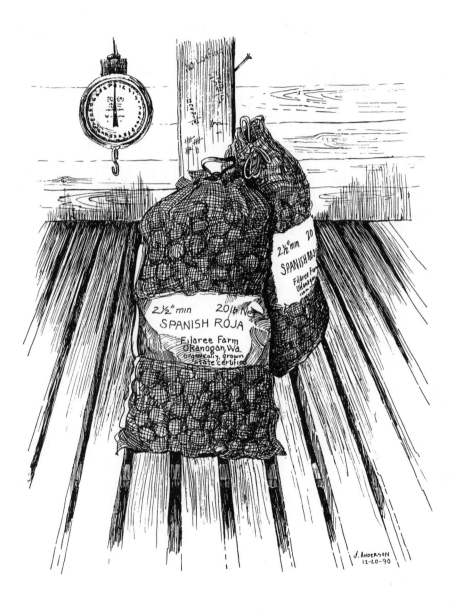

Storage

With proper harvest, curing, and storage conditions, the different types of garlic tend to store for different lengths of time. Under poor storage conditions all types of garlic may sprout or rot together.

In general, we think about 25 percent of the storage life is determined by the way the garlic is grown, harvested, and cured. Another 25 percent is due to the particular type of garlic (i.e which varietal group). The remaining 50 percent is probably determined by storage conditions, including especially temperature, humidity, and air circulation.

General Factors ——————————————

Because ophio garlics are generally difficult to store for long periods, small scale growers often must limit the size of their crop to quantities that can be sold before serious deterioration of the bulbs begins. Swollen root nodules do not directly affect the taste and flavor of garlic (though fussy customers may **believe they do**), but they do indicate that long term storage will no longer be possible. Few produce buyers or stores have storage areas well suited to garlic, so they hesitate to buy garlic with swollen root nodules.

We expect to see some root swelling on our largest bulbs of ophio garlic no later than Thanksgiving. (Growers with more ideal storage conditions may do better.) Our smaller bulbs often hold well past Christmas, but, in "off years," all our ophio bulbs may have swollen root nodules by Thanksgiving. In short, we'd like very much to have most of our ophio garlic shipped out in September and October, and all of it gone prior to Christmas. Then we can fall back on our Artichoke garlics. The point is that we have a limited marketing season for high quality ophio garlics.

Our primary market for ophio garlic is gourmet restaurants. They prefer ophio garlic to Artichoke types because of the higher flavor and easier peeling cloves. They will buy poor quality ophio garlic before resorting to Artichoke garlic, but they obviously don't want moldy or dehydrated bulbs. In high production years when our marketing stretches into the holiday season, long term, on-farm storage becomes a necessity.

Long term storage of garlic remains a mystery to most small scale garlic growers, especially those growing ophio garlics. Of course, the majority of small scale growers sell all their garlic within a few months of harvest and don't ever have to store it. Others, like me, have been experimenting with storage, including "controlled atmosphere" storage, for ten years—and the long term storage of ophio garlics is mostly still a mystery. I do know several key factors, but annual variation in the results always suggests I must still be missing one more key piece to the puzzle.

An important factor, without any doubt, is the quality of the garlic before it's placed in storage. Poorly grown, damaged, or poorly cured garlic cannot be expected to store well regardless of storage conditions. Soft bulbs won't get harder. Diseased bulbs won't be cured. Bruised bulbs won't be healed. All these conditions will get progressively worse in storage.

Individual cloves can't be expected to store as well as whole bulbs. Once popped apart, the integrity of the bulb is lost and individual cloves have a much higher tendency to sprout roots and to begin internal growth of the bud. Clove separation is the equivalent of the breaking apart of the cloves from the mother bulb when bulbs are left in the soil. As the bulb swells open, the true stems of the cloves eventually break free from the true stem of the mother bulbs. This process exposes the true stem of the new clove to temperature and moisture changes that can easily cause the clove to break dormancy.

Technically speaking, garlic does not ever go dormant. It does undergo a "period of rest" during which there is no active growth and the exchange of gases between the clove and the atmosphere is very minimal. Rather than "breaking dormancy" at a specific point in time, the depth or degree of rest gradually decreases. Optimum storage conditions are those that keep the bulbs in a deep state of rest.

The variety of garlic is certainly a factor, although there seem to be occasional differences of opinion about which varieties store best in which climates. We always have the most problems with woody-stemmed ophio garlics, particularly the Rocambole group. All the evidence suggests these garlics have a very short period of natural rest lasting only two to three months. We can stretch that out to six months of "enforced dormancy" in some years, but it seems to require exactly the right conditions both before and during storage as well as a bit of luck.

The Asiatic and Continental groups of ophio garlics (not yet widely grown in North America) commonly store longer than Rocamboles; in fact, they seem to store nearly as long as Artichoke (variety *sativum*) garlics which remain in a state of rest about five to eight months in most years. The Silverskin group varies somewhat. Some years they store about the same as Artichoke garlics. Other years they store ten to twelve months for us. We've had mixed reports from growers in other climatic regions. Some claim that Artichokes are more difficult to store than ophio. The majority report results quite similar to our own.

Humidity

Most growers have far less control over storage humidity than over temperature. High humidity causes the root buds to swell at the base of the individual cloves. After a few weeks of swelling, this condition can be readily observed by examining the bottom of whole bulbs. If the conditions persist, actual root growth can begin. These reactions to high humidity occur regardless of storage temperatures and are largely independent of the state of rest the sprout bud undergoes inside the clove.

Garlic bulbs in excellent and firm condition don't seem to experience root swelling until the humidity reaches 75% to 80%, but, once bulbs suffer moderate dehydration or extended periods of rest, the root swelling seems to occur at even lower humidities of 65% to 75%. Only a few days exposure is necessary to initiate root swell. The process can be greatly slowed if the humidity is significantly reduced, but it cannot be totally stopped.

While we commonly store Artichoke garlics (even as individual cloves) for six months without any swelling of root nodules, our ophio garlics always seem eager to begin root growth. There is variation some years when all the garlic seems to begin the swelling about the same time. We can't explain the variation, but we suspect it may be related to storage temperatures and the conditions the bulbs experienced before storage.

At the opposite extreme, humidity levels below about 40% may cause rapid dehydration of ophio garlics. While variety *sativum* seems nearly immune to the effects of low humidity, most ophio garlics (especially Rocamboles) peel very easily because the clove skins do not adhere tightly to the clove flesh. While easy-peel is a definite plus in marketability, it also makes the bulbs more prone to gradual dehydration. The exchange of gases and vapors between the garlic flesh and the outside environment is simply far more likely to occur and far easier to occur in Rocamboles than in most other garlics.

In the absence of humidity controls, we recommend garlics be stored in a dry, cool environment rather than a moist place. Refrigerators and damp basements are not recommended for long storage not only because of high humidity but because of poor air circulation that tends to favor mold development. A cool attic or a room temperature storage bay in the house—even a cold dry garage—should provide better storage than a moist environment. A small fan on a low speed setting is usually enough to insure good air circulation.

Temperature

Temperatures have a direct effect on the sprouting of the bud inside the clove. Temperatures of forty to fifty degrees Fahrenheit for one to two weeks will initiate sprouting in ophio garlics of the Rocambole group. Other ophio varieties and variety *sativum* garlics seem to require longer exposure to these temperatures—perhaps three to six weeks—but the time frame varies annually. With the exception of planting stock that you want to begin growth, garlic should never be stored between forty and fifty degrees Fahrenheit.

The optimum temperatures for sprouting of garlic are not meant to suggest that cloves will not sprout at higher or lower temperatures. It simply takes longer to bring the garlic out of its state of rest when temperatures are cooler or warmer than the optimum range of forty to fifty degrees Fahrenheit. Garlic stored at fifty to sixty degrees Fahrenheit seems to require two to three times the length of exposure in order to break the state of rest. That's roughly two to four weeks for Rocamboles, and six to twelve weeks for other garlics. Temperatures of thirty-six to thirty-nine degrees Fahrenheit have roughly the same effect as temperatures of fifty to sixty degree Fahrenheit.

Best long term storage seems to occur when storage temperatures are very low (thirty-two to thirty-five degrees Fahrenheit) or close to room temperature (sixty to seventy degrees Fahrenheit). However, these two temperature ranges seem to have very different effects on the garlic **after** it's removed from storage. Garlic stored near room temperature simply continues to pull out of its state of rest very gradually, but garlic stored near freezing seems to end its state of rest quite rapidly once its removed to room temperatures. Many growers report serious clove and bulb deterioration within two to four weeks after garlic is removed from extended cold storage. This suggests that garlic should not be removed from extended cold storage unless it will be shipped to market immediately.

We suspect the rapid deterioration of the state of rest after extended cold storage is caused by two basic factors. One is that humidities in cold storage tend to be very high. Once removed to room temperatures, the bulbs are wet and must be placed in a dry environment for at least several days—sometimes up to one week. This short period of high humidity at relatively high temperatures is often enough to initiate immediate swelling of the root nodules. The sudden and extreme temperature change also has a marked effect on the internal chemistry of the bulb. Release of carbon dioxide increases very rapidly. In effect, the garlic thinks it is springtime and well past the time when growth should begin. The state of rest of the sprout bud which was gradually decreasing even in cold storage is decreased very rapidly when temperatures rise suddenly and dramatically. In short, while cold storage keeps garlic in a deep state of rest, it also apparently negates the need for additional rest after the garlic is removed from cold storage. This makes the value of extended cold storage highly questionable for most small scale garlic growers.

There is an additional problem associated with long cold storage. The high humidity and poor air circulation favor the growth of some fungi that grow well at low temperatures. Some grow on the outer bulb wrappers without causing any real damage, but others may grow on the clove skins inside the bulb wrappers where they are impossible to clean off. Whether such molds actually damage the garlic is immaterial. It's disconcerting when a customer breaks apart a bulb and finds mold.

Short term garlic storage at very low temperatures doesn't seem to present any serious difficulties, but it doesn't gain growers very much either. Given the cost of cold storage (especially in hot weather shortly after harvest), and the fact that garlic seems to store well at room temperature, cold storage is a dubious option. So far as we can tell, commercial garlic growers in North America never felt that cold storage offered enough advantage to offset the cost and the cullage.

Common Storage

All our own experience and all references in the literature suggest that long term storage of table stock is best accomplished with temperatures between about fifty-five and sixty-five degrees Fahrenheit and humidity between 40% and 60%. Good air circulation among individual bulbs is at least as important as temperature and humidity.

Our own warehouse at Filaree Farm may represent as

nearly an ideal environment as is possible, despite (or perhaps because of) the fact it was built in 1917 for common storage of apples. The building has no direct temperature control; instead, it has a slatted floor about two feet off a dirt floor. There are vents in the foundation all around the building, and two large chimneys through the roof that can be opened or closed with trap doors. The indoor temperature is nearly always within two degrees of the mean daily average outdoor temperature, although there is a time lag of several days whenever extreme changes in outdoor temperatures occur. If the outdoor high is one hundred degrees and the overnight low is fifty degrees then the warehouse will likely fluctuate between seventy-three and seventy-seven degrees Fahrenheit.

The indoor temperature can be decreased only when it's cold at night. By opening the vents and chimneys late in the evening or early in the morning a draft is created that sucks warm air out through the roof and replaces it with cold air pulled in through the floor. When outdoor temperatures get too cold (in winter), we build fires in a small woodstove. Despite 1500 square feet of floor space, the building is insulated with sawdust walls one foot thick, so it holds heat well.

Smaller models of our warehouse could be built by many growers at relatively low cost, especially if the building served for storage of cleaned bulbs (which doesn't require much room) rather than for initial curing of the crop. There are drawbacks to this type of building. If it turns rainy during warm weather, we have no good way to keep the humidity from rising. A wood fire in the stove would lower humidity only as it raised temperatures to unacceptably high levels. Luckily, rainy periods aren't common occurrences in our semi-arid climate because the wood and sawdust structure would soak up moisture readily and keep the humidity too high. Growers in humid climates may need a dehumidifier.

It's also hard to maintain good air circulation in winter when the building is closed up tight. We operate fans most of the time and occasionally open the doors in order to replace stale air with fresh air. Low speed fans are very inexpensive to operate.

In some years we experience very warm temperatures (even overnight) all the way through September and October. We suspect this prolonged storage at temperatures that start around seventy-five degrees Fahrenheit and only gradually work their way down to sixty-five degrees Fahrenheit over a four month period when the humidity is often below 40% is the primary reason we have problems with Rocambole garlics dehydrating. The problem is compounded when even a short, rainy period raises the humidity to 70% or 80% so that root nodules begin to swell. Small bulbs and small to medium bulbs grown in relatively poor rather than rich fertile soil definitely store much longer under these conditions. We just accept the fact that the largest bulbs need to be marketed first.

For many small scale growers the best available storage is in a little-used section of the house at (or about ten degrees below) room temperature. Air circulation can be assured by a small fan. Be sure the garlic isn't sitting in direct sunlight by a window. Large amounts of garlic can be troublesome inside the house because of the space required. If stored garlic has to occupy two different areas, be sure to sell the bulbs in the poorest storage area first. If all the garlic is normally sold by October, almost any shed, garage, or outbuilding may be sufficient.

Controlled Atmosphere Storage

In the western United States, the supply of ophio garlic usually runs out about Thanksgiving. Shortly thereafter, large volumes of low quality ophio garlic begin appearing from China and Korea. Later in the winter it may come from Mexico, Chile or Argentina. The price of the imported garlic is amazingly cheap—about one-fifth the cost of our domestic garlic—yet our customers tell us they would prefer to continue buying our garlic despite paying five times the price.

As a result, we started experimenting with "controlled atmosphere" storage of garlic. Controlled atmosphere (CA) storage involves reduced levels of oxygen and increased nitrogen that slow the bulbs metabolism to practically zero and prevent normal rates of deterioration for extended periods. The technology was first applied to apples in our region in the 1960s, and quickly revolution-ized the apple industry by allowing year round marketing of fruit.

Many people (including me) question the quality of so-called "fresh" apples after nine months in CA storage. The industry simply figures that low quality apples in late spring are preferable to no apples at all. The real signifi-cance of CA storage is not that fruit can be held year round; rather, it's that the normal marketing season can be **extended**. If we could extend the marketing season for ophio garlic only two to three months, we could prac-tically double the quantity of garlic we can currently grow, and we could compete head to head with imported ophio garlic through most of the winter.

We discovered in 1988 that scientists in the southeast-ern U.S. had mastered CA storage technology for onions for the first time. Our initial reaction was that garlic should store well in a similar environment, so we teamed up with some local CA experts and built some small test cham-bers.

The 1988-89 experiment was not well controlled be-cause we couldn't afford the expensive automatic monitor-ing equipment. One chamber actually fell to zero percent oxygen for several weeks. The levels of oxygen, nitro-gen, and temperature varied more in the second chamber than we wanted them to. Still, the results were promising.

Our initial goal was to store ophio garlic until the first of January. Actually, we stored some bulbs until the mid-dle of April. They came out of storage in nearly the same condition that they went into storage eight months earlier, but they also deteriorated very rapidly. Garlic removed from storage in November, however, stored well the rest of the winter in common storage in our warehouse.

We placed three types of bulbs into our first test cham-bers—freshly dug whole plants, uncleaned bulbs cured only one week and then topped, and cleaned bulbs fully cured. Upon removal, nearly all the uncleaned bulbs and plants had mold on the outer bulb surfaces. We assumed these were soil fungi associated with the dirt on the bulbs. Cleaned bulbs had no exterior molds but did tend to have small amounts of mold on the clove skins inside the bulb. None of the molds appeared to cause any direct harm to the garlic, and they all cleaned off easily or disappeared after a few days at room temperatures.

Bulbs that experienced zero percent oxygen levels for two weeks suffered death of the sprout bud and began rotting at the base of the clove within one to two weeks after removal from storage. The rest of the bulbs dried down well and remained very firm for three to four weeks, but began to sport brown discolored flesh within ten to fourteen days despite remaining very firm. Overall, the results were better than we had expected, but not good enough to warrant large volume storage of garlic.

In 1989-90, we raised the temperature two degrees and lowered the nitrogen levels slightly. More importantly, instead of taking the bulbs out of CA directly to room temperature in mid-winter, we transferred the bulbs from CA to common cold storage, at thirty-four degrees Fahrenheit for two weeks before placing bulbs at room temperature. This scenario resulted in the best quality garlic, some of which stored an additional six months at room temperature. But the percentage of cull bulbs was still much higher than we were used to seeing in the normal storage garlic marketed in fall and early winter.

Like any new technology, CA storage of garlic has a lot of little quirks. It will probably require five to ten years of testing to really perfect the procedure, but we're confident enough that we hope to test market small quantities of CA garlic by 1992. CA rooms are expensive to build, but not too costly to maintain and operate after the initial investment. In general, the technology seems to show far more promise than ordinary cold storage of garlic.

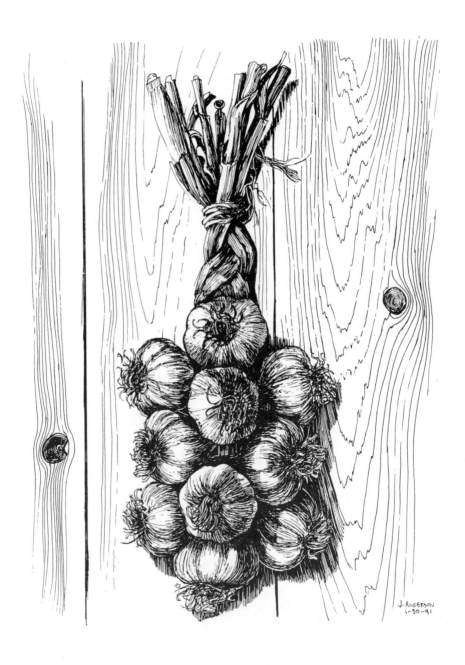

Marketing

Marketing of farm produce involves an age-old dilemma. It's not enough just to grow the crop. Farmers also have to sell the crop, or pay someone else to do it for them. Most modern farmers choose the latter route, and that's one reason so many farmers are no longer in business. It's not cheap to have other people do our work for us.

One Man's Story

When James Donaldson and friends at Libby Creek Farm began growing Spanish Roja garlic in the mid-1970s, garlic in America was still largely synonymous with Gilroy, California. This was ironic because the majority of "fresh" garlic in America was imported every year. The average price per pound to American farmers was between forty and eighty cents—a price slightly higher than what was commonly paid for imported garlic twenty years ago. The entire fresh market garlic industry in America seemed structured around low quality, mass produced bulbs from foreign nations with very cheap and very vast labor forces. In order to compete, the majority of American garlic was machine cultivated and harvested in order to be competitively priced.

James Donaldson was a visionary. He recognized the superior flavor of the Rocambole garlic he was growing, and he knew that neither California softneck garlic (selected largely on the basis of productivity per acre, processibility, and storageability) nor foreign imports could hold a candle to his handcrafted, organically grown, gourmet bulbs. He also realized that Rocamboles could not be well grown in California; in fact, Okanogan County in Wash-

ington state had a more perfect combination of soil and
climate than almost anywhere else in the world.

These discoveries didn't come easily. James first had
to prove that Rocamboles could be northern grown by fall
planting when all the experts promised that such garlic
would winterkill in northern Washington state. He had to
prove that Okanogan soils and climate could produce superior garlic bulbs when the established brokers and distributors all believed garlic could only be grown in California. In fact, most of them didn't know what ophio garlics
even were.

The   obstacles seemed insurmountable. How could a
rundown, knapweed-infested farm in northern Washington
state (a farm that had never before grown garlic) compete
against Gilroy, California, and giants such as the famous
Christopher Ranch?

James Donaldson also realized Libby Creek Farm could
not and did not need to compete with Gilroy, California,
or the imported garlic. What was the point when James
intended to grow gourmet garlic, and Gilroy was mostly
producing bulbs for processing? There was no comparison. The only question was where to begin.

That brings me to several of the other qualities of
James Donaldson. James began with his great love and
respect for the land and for farmers. To understand how
and why James Donalson developed a somewhat unique
marketing scheme for garlic, it may be helpful to know
that James was born one-quarter Cherokee Indian in rural
Oklahoma. He understood the dilemmas of farmers, laborers, poor people, and rural Americans in general. As a
youth he witnessed the deterioration of "grandfather's
creeks" when the Osage Hills above the Cherokee lands
were sold to the Sinclairs and Rockefellers—the byprod-
ucts of the new oil wells eventually "salted" the creeks
and severely impacted the fish and wildlife on the Cherokee lands.

The ethics of James's marketing scheme were partly
due to his training as a minister, yet he quickly outgrew
the anachronistic restraints of both the modern church
and traditional Judeo-Christian theology. What he hung
onto afterwards was compassion, even when he learned
to think in terms of shifting cultural paradigms and evolu-

tionary (rather than simple historical) processes. James's upbringing resulted in a unique view of small scale farmers.

"We're not simple laborers or traditional farmers," he reasoned. "We're refugees of a dying Industrial Age. We recognize the rural roots and origins of our modern urban culture, and we are here today to raise the voices of battered agricultural lands, to repair the damage to our soils, our families, our communities, and our culture. As such, we are worthy citizens. We will be paid an honest wage, and we will be paid enough that we can continue the regeneration of our soil, families, and communities. Let it begin here in this soil, but let us also bridge the gap that bleeds like an ancient gaping wound between urban and rural people. Let us seek support in the form of an honest wage from those few people who have both the money to purchase our garlic and the understanding of who we are and what we are doing."

In short, James Donaldson set the price of his gourmet garlic at $2.50 per pound—three times the going price—and set out to ***personally*** contact as many people from his more recent urban past as possible. He also began a list of environmental, feminist, eco-theological, anti-nuclear, and just plain progressive networks because he believed all of them had good reason to be his allies. Finally, he began visiting the chefs at gourmet restaurants in the Pacific Northwest.

More than anything else, James Donaldson was a communicator. He brought people together who never dreamed they had anything in common, and then created enduring friendships and alliances. He motivated people who thought all hope was lost. He teased out hidden talents and skills from desperate individuals with no sense of purpose. And, he sold high-priced, gourmet garlic to all of them.

James did not work alone, mind you. While he was the inspiration and drive, Bob Elk, David Granatstein, and Loren Hager did most of the legwork, field work, and hands-on research. Libby Creek Farm was a community in which everyone played an important role. James Donalson simply stood out as a man with a vision.

The rest is history, so to speak. The reputation of

Spanish Roja garlic eventually spread all along the west coast. The reputation of Okanogan County garlic growers as producers of top quality Rocambole garlic also spread. Within ten years, produce buyers in California were sending semitrucks northward with these simple instructions—"Buy all the garlic you can find, as long as it's grown in Okanogan County."

In his own unique way, James Donaldson did what any good marketer should do. He promoted his garlic as unique, uncommon, and special compared to everyone else's—and, indeed, it was. He associated the product with a geographical place and region that could be easily recognized and remembered. He associated both the garlic and the place with a purpose and a destiny. And, he sought out specific people and markets rather than advertising to average consumers. He knew that his "chosen few" would eventually spread both the word and the habit to "average" American consumers.

Stated another way, James refused to beg. He never called typical garlic brokers and asked "What will you pay for my garlic today, sir?" He never sold garlic at the "going price" because that would have typed his garlic as common and ordinary. He refused to play the typical economic mind-game known as supply and demand. Instead, he created a new game with new rules. It was a game based on worth and value rather than cost or price. It was based on quality rather than quantity, and on customers rather than anonymous consumers. It was based on nurturing rather than exploitation, and on common bonds rather than traditional boundaries. James created healthy relationships rather than being gobbled up by traditional structures.

Ground Rules

Times have changed since the seventies. Small scale garlic production is now quite popular and competition is stiff, especially among northern growers. Local markets are often flooded in the fall and early winter. Yet, the basic ground rules have not changed. Assuming that you've already mastered the fine art of growing great garlic, how should you market your crop in the 1990s?

First, know your product and what makes it special. You need to be knowledgeable and you need to be a good communicator. If the latter skill just isn't up your alley, then consider finding a broker who understands the value of your small farm and your product.

Second, choose your market (i.e. the target audience). Who, specifically, are you catering to? Possibilities include:

- local stores and local customers (especially in rural America),
- specialty outlets such as organic food co-ops, novelty shops, delicatessens, and farmers' markets,
- gourmet restaurants,
- ethnic communities,
- specialty food processors with gourmet product lines,
- brokers and wholesalers.

If your garlic has planting stock value, then add:

- new northern garlic growers,
- established southern growers who need to rejuvenate their planting stock,
- collectors,
- researchers.

Also consider direct, on-farm sales and mail order sales. Consider garlic products such as fresh greens, fresh garlic spears, garlic powder, pickled garlic cloves, garlic extracts, garlic braids, garlic wreaths, and garlic pendants. Each product targets a slightly different audience and demands different packaging, different promotion, and different pricing. If you decide to market both bulk garlic and specialty products, don't package them both in the same plain brown wrapper. Choose a package that is suitable for the value of the product. Remember that nice packaging can actually increase the value of specialty products (e.g. gift packs).

The Finer Points

Choose a farm name and design and print an effective label and logo. Print a brochure or flyer describing who you are and what you offer. Print a price list so that buyers know in advance what the product will cost. Develop a mailing list so that old customers are never forgotten.

Design and print small farm cards so that people (even casual acquaintances) have easy access to you via mail or phone. Print order forms to make it easy for customers to place orders. Print invoices with your farm name, address, and phone number. Choose packaging that is standard in size and easy to ship and handle, yet distinctive and memorable in appearance. Finally, ship only top quality products. Mercilessly cull out less than perfect bulbs. Give the customer the benefit of the doubt.

Lastly, work your tail off. If you thought the last two pages sounded like a lot of work, hold on to your hat because you haven't even punched the time clock yet. Marketing will be a full time enterprise, every bit as time consuming as garlic growing. It requires skills quite different from traditional farming skills. In particular, it requires interfacing with a lot of very busy (often harried) urban professionals whose lifestyles, values, and skills are likely totally different than your own.

Marketing skills can be developed—you don't have to be born with the knack—but many small farmers will decide it's just too much work to pile on top of the already busy farm routine. If so, find a broker. Good brokers are more than just good business people. They're also thoroughly human. They should be approached the same way you'd approach a produce buyer or gourmet chef. Talk to them, in person if possible. Take samples of your garlic and your packaging. Have price sheets and shipping costs in hand. But, above all, be prepared to communicate who you are and what you have to offer.

The trick is to speak both warmly and concisely. You have to sound knowledgeable and confident without sounding arrogant or groveling. You need to tell your story, but you can't waste the buyer's time either. Be well-prepared. You'll probably know very quickly whether or not you're making a good impression. If not, you should cut your visit short. Your goal, however, is still to get the buyer to agree to try an initial shipment. If you think it's important to access the market through a particular broker, you might offer to ship a free sample carton of twenty or forty pounds with the first shipment.

Scope

Be sure to tailor your appetite to the volume of garlic you can actually produce. It's not wise to try to break into a large market if you only have a few hundred pounds of garlic to offer. (Consider pooling your product with other local growers) It's an even greater mistake to depend on one or two small outlets to market a crop of 5,000 pounds when they commonly sell only fifty pounds of garlic per week each.

Start by calculating how many pounds per week and month you need to ship in order to move all the garlic by a target date. If you can start shipping September 1st and want to be finished by November 30th, then a 5,000 pound crop needs to move out at a rate of approximately 1600 pounds per month, or 400 pounds per week. Seek out appropriate markets and be sure they understand that your season of availability is basically only three months for ophio garlics—September through November—or longer for soft necks..

Contact and Perseverance

If you're marketing direct, don't be afraid to call a produce buyer just to check in with him or her. Ask if the last shipment arrived in good condition. Ask if the product is selling well. Ask if the buyer is pleased with your product or not. In short, seek feedback.

Don't be depressed if you get rejected a lot. It's usually not personal, and you shouldn't take it personally. Many produce buyers already have dependable sources and simply can't be bothered with small farmers. Perseverance is the motto of all small farmers marketing their own crops, so don't expect the job to be easy.

Generally speaking, the fresh garlic market in America has barely been tapped in a few large metropolitan areas. The mass marketplace still hasn't been touched, but it may begin to show interest during the current decade. Some shopping habits and preferences are changing in ways that will encourage typical consumers to pay more attention to quality and varietal differences. The fluctuating but, nevertheless, increased interest in organically grown foods is an example. The slow move away from Red Delicious apples to more expensive but better tasting new varieties is another.

Other Garlic Products

The market for specialty products is especially wide open right now. If you're located close enough to urban markets, there is beginning to be interest in fresh garlic greens and fresh garlic spears. Some Oriental ethnic groups have always sought out these highly perishable products, but a few gourmet restaurants and specialty shops are now also seeking them out.

Garlic greens can be grown from planted or broadcast cloves, whole bulbs, or bulbils. Bulbils probably work out best because the green shoot is small and guaranteed to remain succulent longer than greens from cloves and bulbs. The latter must be harvested early in the spring because leaves become chewy when they get too big.

Garlic greens are highly perishable. When grown from bulbils, whole plants are dug, washed, and bundled in bunches of ten to twenty-five plants. Roots are sometimes trimmed, but the greens stay fresh better if roots are left intact and kept constantly moist. Immediate cooling or refrigeration is usually required, and the greens need to reach the market within twenty-four hours. Gourmet restaurants and produce buyers may take regular shipments on particular days of the week. Growers can then make the rounds several times a week.

When properly packaged in a high humidity container after initial cooling, fresh greens are sometimes sent UPS to their destination. You'll have to communicate well with the local UPS people to ensure the best shipping days and fastest routes. You can even contract with UPS to make regular farm pickups at predetermined times and days.

Fresh garlic spears from topsetting ophio garlics have been popular in oriental dishes for millennia. The spears should be harvested as soon as possible after they first appear, though some buyers prefer six to twelve inch stems as well. The immature spears are less perishable than garlic greens, but they're still a delicacy that immediately needs to be cooled, moistened, and transported. Garlic spears need to be grown from cloves or bulbs since bulbils are usually too small to produce topsets. Cloves can be either fall or spring planted. Spears appear in very late May or early to mid-June in most locations regardless of the planting date. When spears are taken from fall-planted cloves, the main crop of garlic bulbs can also be harvested a month later. Spears can also be ground up in a food blender and used to make delicious pasta.

We know of at least one grower currently experimenting with spear production from a semi-perennial planting of garlic. Cloves or whole bulbs are planted, spears are harvested, and the plants are left in the ground to mature and regrow the following year. Semi-perennial garlic might be risky for some growers. Weed control could be difficult. More importantly, mold and disease problems could become serious since the garlic isn't rotated to new ground. We still think it's worth trying.

Ambitious growers in the right location have the opportunity to market fresh garlic greens in the spring, fresh garlic spears in late spring, and traditional dried bulbs in late summer and early fall. Special skills, timing, and handling are obviously required for the greens and spears, but any market gardeners already selling fresh greens should handle the tasks easily.

Dried Products

You may decide not to harvest and market fresh garlic spears, but don't throw the spears away. Dried spears, especially Rocambole spears allowed to fully coil, are very unique in appearance and quite useful in dried floral arrangements. Both wholesalers and retailers sometimes buy them in bulk, tied in bunches of ten to fifty, for prices varying from ten to twenty-five cents per spear.

Dried garlic spears are generally used sparingly in dried floral arrangements.One or two spears can serve as an unusual conversation piece rising serpent-like behind the right combination of flowers, or it can serve as a centerpiece. Dried spears can also be woven into braids and wreaths by soaking the stems in water until they become pliable. Decorative wreaths can even be made entirely of garlic spears if a few red peppers, evergreen sprigs, or dried flowers are added for color, texture, and balance.

Garlic braids have long been the most popular dried garlic product. All types of garlic can be braided, but ophio garlics (as usual) require a little extra skill and planning because of the woody stem. Garlic plants are normally **partially** cured (enough to prevent molding of the stem and leaves), then quickly braided while the stems are still pliable. Ophio garlics for braiding need to be harvested a few days ahead of the main ophio crop. After several days of curing, the woody stems need to be "broken" at one inch intervals along the stem by bending them over between the thumb and forefinger. The term "broken" is actually misleading. "Bent" may be more appropriate, but "broken" is the term used nonetheless. If woody stems are too dry, they really do break and that's not the desired result. Braiders need pliable necks so the stems need to be "bent" at just the right stage of dryness.

Garlic braids come in all shapes and sizes from single row to triple row, and from one foot to twelve foot lengths. A few people like large-bulbed braids (which are harder to make), but most prefer medium-sized bulbs and moderate braid lengths so that finished braids don't weigh more than a few pounds each. Silverskins are still the most popular garlics for braiding because they already have soft necks and they store longer than most other garlics. But, we've seen a lot of interest lately in braided Artichoke and ophio garlics which bring higher prices because they're harder to make.

I've always thought that braids look nicer and sell better when they are moderately decorated with a few dried flowers. The floral additions should not be so ostentatious they hide the garlic bulbs. Their purpose is to soften the overall appearance by complimenting the bulb shape and color. Braids also sell better when they have braided cords (of yarn or sisal) to facilitate hanging the braid. A small card dangling by a short string can add color and style (if it's well designed) while also advertising your farm name.

Garlic wreaths are now rivalling braids in some urban markets, especially during the holiday season from Thanksgiving to Christmas. Wreaths generally incorporate garlic bulbs into a main structure of other materials, but we've also seen whole garlic wreaths. While wreaths tend to be decoratively used, even more so than braids, they can also be made to facilitate the easy removal of garlic bulbs for kitchen use. Wreaths generally need to include more colorful combinations of material than do braids.

Most growers sell braids and wreaths at a per each price, but they calculate the price based on the actual pounds of garlic bulbs and the labor hours and packaging requirements. Good braiders can turn out three or four beautiful braids per hour, but wreaths require more artistic flavor and better packaging if they are to be mailed or shipped. Braids seem to sell best when priced between $8 and $15 each, but $30 wreaths are not uncommon.

Processed Products

Garlic powder is the best known garlic product. The majority of Americans still prefer garlic powder to raw garlic because its quick and easy to use and store. That's why so much California garlic is dehydrated.

Gourmet garlic powder sells well in specialty markets versus ordinary food stores. Consumers are willing to pay higher prices (e.g. $8 to $12 per pound) because they know the powder is hand ground from organically grown bulbs. We always end up with lots of bulbs that have one bad clove. It can't be shipped as a partial bulb, but the remaining cloves really are of gourmet quality.

Individual cloves must be peeled and sliced into thin strips which are dried at 110 degrees Fahrenheit for about three days before grinding. An Oregon man recently invented a blower that peels garlic by blasting air around it. Slicing is then also done by machinery.

The garlic powder can be sold by the quart or gallon to food co-ops, or placed in small two to three ounce herb jars with attractive home made labels. The work is tedious, but a good way for some small scale farmers to pass the winter hours around a kitchen wood stove. Some farmers even throw "garlic peeling" parties, which is a great idea if you have the drying racks to accommodate a lot of sliced garlic pieces at one time.

Dehydrated garlic in a powder is also the favorite form

of garlic desired by herb companies that use garlic as one of the ingredients in various herbal remedies and medicines. These companies pay very high prices for organically grown garlic powder guaranteed free of residues, and they often contract with growers. Some of them prefer whole bulbs they can send to their own dehydrating or processing facilities. Either way, the herbal and medicinal markets for garlic are growing very rapidly.

Garlic oil is a very valuable commodity in short supply. It's sometimes used in cooking, but also in medicine. Oil can be obtained from whole bulbs or from the fresh cut spears of ophio garlics. The few companies in need of garlic oil will likely be very fussy about the quality and oil content of the product they buy. This specialty market usually requires on farm inspections by specialists who contract crops grown to their exact specifications.

Finally, processed garlic products can include specialty food items such as pickled garlic cloves. Pickled garlic is commonly imported from the Orient and sold in specialty shops for $10 to $15 per half pint. This is not a favorite American snack food, but it's well worth investigating if you know of any import stores offering this type of gourmet food product.

Summary

As you can see, the possibilities are quite broad and varied. America needs more garlic entrepreneurs willing to experiment with new products. Some gourmet foods and floral arrangements are extremely "trendy"—they're popular this year and out of vogue next year—but beneath the somewhat fashionable possibilities lies a solid and steadily growing market for almost any kind of garlic food product. We currently live in a health conscious culture as well as a relatively wealthy culture (i.e. both the interest and the money is there). It's up to innovative growers to invent creative avenues of access to the consumers' stomach, psyche, and pocketbook. Why limit yourself to just one of the angles? On the other hand, don't tackle too many tasks at once. Quantity and variety are not substitutes for quality—at least, not for long. Learn to grow great garlic first and foremost. Then, whatever you do, do it well.

A Closing Note
About Garlic Taste

Individual preferences vary widely, and no two people describe the same garlic taste despite tasting the exact same clove. In addition, there are substantial differences among individual garlic strains, and individual strains will taste different each year in accordance with varying climatic factors. Even the amount of rainfall and differences in soil texture and fertility can significantly affect taste, and so can the length of time in storage.

But garlic taste is even more complex than the myriad variations described in the previous paragraph. For starters, its a combination of factors including primarily **taste** and **aroma**, but also appearance and texture. Taste and aroma combine to produce **flavor**. There is also the **aftertaste**--the lingering flavor that remains after the initial taste is dissipated. Finally, there are several kinds of taste. The **reflex taste**, which is not a true taste, is very significant in garlic. Its the initial reaction to burning hotness. If reflex tastes are very strong then other **true tastes**, such as sweetness, can be almost completely overpowered.

Let me share a story with you to illustrate the complexities of garlic taste. We've grown Spanish Roja garlic (subspecies *ophioscorodon*, variety Rocambole) at Filaree Farm for fifteen years. During that time, Spanish Roja never lost a single taste test. Gourmet tasters even correctly identified Spanish Roja grown at Filaree Farm and distinguished it from the same garlic strain grown in other states.

In 1989, we sent a few garlic samples, including Spanish Roja, back east for taste tests. Though it was not an official taste test, Spanish Roja was once again preferred by a majority of tasters.

In 1990, we sent nineteen different garlic strains for testing. This time, Spanish Roja finished ninth in overall flavor, twelfth in raw flavor, and fourth in roasted flavor. The results were certainly a disappointment, but also perhaps misleading. In fact, with few exceptions, softneck garlics generally rated very high in the 1990 tests compared to ophio garlics.

In retrospect, the results can probably be explained by weather. The winter of 1989-90 was the mildest in recorded history in our location. January temperatures reached sixty degrees several times. No really cold weather occurred except for two weeks in February. It rained instead of snowed all winter. March and April turned hot and dry when we should have gotten spring rains. Consequently, the garlic grew slowly all winter (instead of resting) and was then actually stressed during the months it normally grows most vigorously.

Finally, the rains came in May and June during the time our garlic was supposed to be bulbing and experiencing very warm or hot temperatures. Nor were these typical rains for our semiarid region. It actually rained twenty-seven out of thirty-five days and nearly rotted the garlic.

In many ways, our 1989-90 winter was the kind one would expect on the coast in the maritime Pacific Northwest, a region well suited to softneck garlics, but not ophio garlics. We suspect that's why Spanish Roja performed so poorly in the 1990 taste tests.

The lesson is simple. No one person, no single taste test, and no single growing season will accurately reflect the taste of any garlic strain. Garlic requires several years to acclimate itself, and then the taste will still vary annually on the basis of at least a dozen or more variables. In many ways, garlic taste is just as deceptively simple as the garlic plant. Don't judge too harshly on the basis of first impressions.

Bibliography

Books

Airola, Paavo O., 1984, *The Miracle of Garlic*, Health Plus Publishers, Phoenix.

Astley, D., N.L. Innes, and Q.P. vander Meer, 1982, *Genetic Resources of Allium Species*, International Board for Plant Genetic Resources, Rome.

Bailey, L.H., and E.Z. Bailey, 1976, *Hortus Third*, revised and expanded by the staff of Liberty Hyde Bailey Hortorium, Cornell University, MacMillan Publishing Co., New York.

Candolle, Alphonse de, 1908, *The Origins of Cultivated Plants*, D. Appleton Co., New York.

Fernald, H.T., and Harold H. Shepard, 1942, *Applied Entomology*, McGraw-Hill Book Co., Inc., New York.

Harris, Lloyd J., 1979, *The Book of Garlic*, Aris Books, Addison-Wesley Publishing Co., Inc., 3rd rev. ed., paperback, Berkeley, California.

Jones, Henry A., and Louis K. Mann, 1963, *Onions and Their Allies: Botany, Cultivation and Utilization*, Interscience Publishers, Inc., New York.

Metcalf, C.L., and R.L. Metcalf, 1951, *Destructive and Useful Insects: Their Habits and Control*, McGraw-Hill Book Co., Inc., New York.

Simons, Paul, 1980, *Garlic, The Healing Herb*, Thorsons Publishers Ltd.., Wellingborough, Northamptonshire, Great Britain.

Sturtevant, E. Louis, edited by U.P. Hedrick, 1972, *Sturtevant's Edible Plants of the World*, Dover Publishers, Inc., New York.

The Times Concise Atlas of World History, edited by Geoffrey Barraclough, 1985, Hammond Inc., Maplewood, New Jersey.

Articles

Couto, F. AD'A, 1956, "Symptoms of Mineral Deficiency in Garlic," *Proceedings of the American Society of Horticultural Science*, 68:358-365.

Greathead, Arthur S., June 1978, "Control of Penicillium Decay of Garlic," *California Agriculture*, p 18.

Liu, H.J., F.I. McEwen, and G. Ritcey, June 1982, "Forecasting Events in the Life Cycle of the Onion Maggot, *Hylema antiqua* (Diptera: Anthomyiidae): Application to Control Schemes," Entomological Society of America, *Environmental Entomology*, II:751-755.

Mann, Louis K., and David A. Lewis, October 1956, "Rest and Dormancy in Garlic," *Hilgardia*, University of California, Berkeley, 26(3): 161-189.

Sussman, Vic, September 1985, "Garlic Unveiled," *Organic Gardening*, pp 46-54.

Tyler, Kent B. et al, March-April 1988, "Diagnosing Nutrient Need of Garlic," *California Agriculture*, 42(2): 28-29.

Other References

Abstract 2422, April 1990, *Horticultural Abstracts*, 60(4): 280.

Antonelli, Arthur, and Dan Mayer, July 1983, "The Onion Maggot in the Home Garden," Extension Bulletin 1180, Washington State University Cooperative Extension, Pullman, Washington.

Brammall, Dr. Ron, "Garlic Production in Ontario—Improved Prospects," Horticultural Experiment Station, Simcoe, Ontario.

European Economic Community, "The EEC Common Quality Standards for Garlic," Annex IV, abstracted from regulation No. 10/65/EEC, pp. 35-38.

Kline, Roger A., and The Garlic Seed Foundation of New York State, 1989 (rev. 3/90), "Garlic," Vegetable Crops Report 387, Cornell University, Ithaca, New York.

Komissarov, V.A., translated by John F. Swenson, 1964, "On the Evolution of Cultivated Garlic, [*A. sativum* L.], Proceedings of Timirjazov Agricultural Academy, No. 4: pp. 70-73.

Seelig, R.A., April 1974, "Fruit and Vegetable Facts and Pointers," United Fresh Fruit and Vegetable Association, Washington, D.C., (2nd completely new edition).

University of California, Dec. 1976, "Growing Garlic in California," Leaflet 2948, Agricultural Extension Service, Davis, California, rev.

University of Illinois Cooperative Extension, June 1966, "Onion Maggot," NHE-50, Urbana, Illinois.

Washington State University Cooperative Extension, April 1977, "White Rot of Onions," EM 4202, Pullman, Washington.

Glossary

Allicin—one of the major sulphur-containing breakdown products of the amino acid "cysteine." Allicin is mildly garlic-like and unstable; it quickly breaks down into diallyl disulphide which is the major cause of garlic odor. Allicin and its ingredients have antibacterial properties and the ability to influence the way that lipid fats are broken down in the liver and bloodstream.

ARS—Agricultural Research Station of the United States Department of Agriculture.

Artichoke—common name for any softneck or partial bolting garlic of the *sativum* subspecies in which three or more layers of cloves form a whorl in the fashion of an artichoke plant. The author uses the term "Artichoke" to refer more specifically to a distinct variety of sativum garlics which he calls variety *semisagittalus*; this variety often forms a partial flower stalk and produces bulbils out the side of the false stem.

Asiatic—the common name applied by the author to the specific variety of ophio garlic named "pekinense" (an unconfirmed variety). Asiatic may also refer to the general climatic region of China and Mongolia.

Axil—the upper angle between a leaf and the plant stem; in the case of garlic, the leaves are attached to the stem at the base of the bulb (below ground), and the axil is at the top of the basal plate where cloves are attached.

Basal Plate—the bottom portion (underside) of the true stem (ie., the very hard and scabrous surface at the bottom of the clove or bulb which has root buds located around its outer edge).

Beak—the narrowest tip of the fruit or seed; for garlic, the elongated spear extending from the spathe that encloses the aerial bulbils in a capsule at the top of the flower stalk.

Beltsville—a USDA Agricultural Research Station and Plant Introduction Station in Maryland.

Bitter Garlic—the off-taste often associated with garlic cloves that have begun active growth (i.e., elongation) of the sprout leaf inside the clove, a process often accompanied by some dehydration, by yellowing of the clove flesh and increased emissions of carbon dioxide, and by eventual greening of the sprout leaf. While many people would agree that the taste changes somewhat, many would disagree strongly with use of the term "bitter."

Blade—the more or less expanded portion of the leaf; in garlic, the upper portion of the leaf which grows out away from the false stem.

Blossoming—a term sometimes used to describe varying degrees of bulb overmaturity in which the individual cloves begin to push away from the center so that the bulb begins to open up in the fasion of a blossoming flower. Blossomed bulbs are considered too overmature for table stock, but some blossoming may be desirable for planting stock.

Bolt—produce a flower stalk and bulbils at the expense of further development of the rest of the plant. New leaves are initiated in garlic after the flower stalk begins to grow, but the leaves do not develop very much (i.e., vegetative growth basically ends). Bolting is usually a response to hot weather.

Breaking the Neck—a term used by braiders referring to the process of bending the necks of ophio garlics back and forth at about one inch intervals in order to make them pliable and braidable. The necks are not actually "broken" unless the woody stems are too dry and brittle in which case they are first soaked in water. The same term may apply to the bending over of plant tops in the field in order to force dry-down before harvest.

Bud (i.e., vegetative bud)—an undeveloped leafy shoot, called a sprout after it begins to grow.

Bulb—a swollen and rounded underground stem with thick persistent fleshy scales known as cloves, and dry thin outer scales known as bulb skins or wrappers. The cloves are actually small bulbs themselves but are rarely referred to as such.

Bulb Wrapper—the thin, dry outer scales, sometimes called bulb skins or protective leaves, that occur as several thin and papery layers around the mature dried bulb. Bulb wrappers are specialized portions of the leaf sheaths.

Bulbil—small, usually aerial, secondary cloves often produced in the flower cluster in place of flowers.

CA Storage (Controlled Atmosphere Storage)—a modified storage environment with reduced levels of oxygen and increased levels of nitrogen in order to greatly slow plant metabolism and preserve the quality of stored foods for periods of from four to ten months.

Character—the basic biological traits that are highly hereditable (i.e., genetic).

Clone—any group of individuals produced vegetatively from a single ancestor. Susanville garlic is believed to be a clone of a single mutated bulb of California Early.

Clove Skin—the hard, thick sheath that tightly surrounds the fleshy clove; technically, it is composed of a specialized leaf sheath that lignifies (hardens) in order to protect the clove (another specialized leaf sheath) from physical injury and moisture loss, as well as insect and disease entry. Despite its stubborn adherence to the clove in many garlics, the clove skin is a totally separate leaf that is not biologically connected or attached directly to the clove in any way.

Continental—refers to a general climatic region associated with the arid summers and long, cold winters of south central Asia and the steppe regions that extend into south eastern Europe. It is also the common name applied by the author to a specific variety of ophio garlic often identified by very tall flower stalks, small yellow spathes, tiny bulbils, four to eight cloves per bulb, slightly elongated clove skin tips, and the absence of a tight coil in the flower stalk.

Cold Storage—storage at temperatures below forty degrees Fahrenheit, and often below thirty-four degrees Fahrenheit, for extended periods. The cold temperature is usually maintained by refrigeration equipment.

Common Storage—long term storage of garlic without any refrigeration or mechanized temperature controls.

Corm—on elephant garlic, the small corms are secondary stem swellings formed from secondary buds on the surface of the bulb. Corms are enclosed in very hard, nut-like shells with a sharp point at the top. They should be soaked in water several days to soften the shells before planting.

Cultigen—any cultivated plant or variety of plant of unknown or obscure origins. Technically, all named garlics are cultigens rather than cultivars, but the term is considered esoteric by lay people; thus, I promote the use of the term "strain" in place of cultigen.

Cultivar—a plant variety produced by selective breeding; since garlic produces no true seed and cannot be bred, the technically correct term is "cultigen."

Cysteine—the sulphur-containing amino acid responsible for much of the pungency of garlic after the walls of the tissue cells are disrupted. Before disruption, cysteine is stable and odorless.

Day length sensitivity—technically known as "photoperiodicity," day length sensitivity is the response of plants to the specific number of daylight hours associated with various latitudes. When moved great distances either north or south, daylight sensitive garlics may grow poorly, bolt and mature early, or fail to mature. All garlic is believed to be day length sensitive though not nearly so much as onions. Specific research has not been done.

Dieback (of leaf tips)—the gradual yellowing and browning of the leaf tips; the phenomenon may be caused by frost, disease, nutrient deficiency, insect attack or the onset of plant maturity.

Drip Irrigation—any watering system that applies a very low volume of water at very low pressure to specific individual points of application rather than spraying water over a large area.

Double Clove (or "Doubled Clove")—a single fleshy storage leaf (or clove) that encloses more than one vegetative bud and sprout leaf. The exact cause is unknown. When planted, double cloves yield two flat-sided bulbs. Doubles can sometimes be recognized during clove popping by their odd shape or by irregular vertical depressions or actual cavities down a side of the clove flesh.

Double Row Staggered—a pattern of planting in which double rows are planted several inches apart while the individual cloves are staggered from one row to the next so that any three adjacent cloves form a triangle.

Elliptical—widest at the center and curving together at both ends. Ophio bulbs may be elliptical in shape when they have an odd number of cloves. Many Silverskins and some Artichoke bulbs are shaped elliptically when grown in poor soils.

Endemic—naturally occurring within a certain region or body.

False Seedstalk—a technically correct term sometimes used instead of "flower stalk." The seedstalk is "false" because no true seed is formed.

False Stem—refers to the central portion of the leafy plant, but what gives the appearance of a stem in garlic is actually composed of stout leaf sheaths that are wrapped around each other. The "true stem" of garlic is extremely short and entirely below ground.

Fertile Leaf—a foliage leaf in which fertile buds in the leaf axil at the top of the true stem actually swell into cloves as the bulb matures. Most ophio garlics have only two fertile leaves, but softneck garlics may have from two to twelve depending on climate, variety, and specific strain. So-called "infertile buds" (buds which rarely develop) may occur in the axils of other leaves which are then termed "infertile leaves."

Finished Double—two or more cloves inside a single clove skin, but the fleshy cloves are completely differentiated and not attached to each other. Finished doubles may be planted, but they usually have small true stems that result in smaller, less vigorous plants.

Fresh Market Garlic—high quality, dried bulbs sold to market after full curing but before the end of the garlic's natural period of rest. The term is most frequently applied to ophio garlics whose short period of natural rest usually requires them to be marketed within two to four months of harvest.

Fungus—large group of plants without flowers, leaves or chlorophyll which reproduce by spores or division and get their nourishment from living or dead organic matter. Garlic is highly susceptible to many fungal infections during both growth and storage.

Garlic—from the Anglo-Saxon "gar" meaning lance and "leac" meaning potherb. A bulb-bearing edible plant of the *Allium* Genus.

Gatersleben—the national genebank repository at Gatersleben, formerly in East Germany.

Grade—refers to the degree of quality of commercial garlic bulbs. The United States has only one grade called "U.S. #1." California has its own grades. International grades are "Extra, Class I, and Class II." See also "Size Grade."

Grading—the process of analyzing individual garlic bulbs to determine their overall quality, including firmness, shape, cleanliness, damage, edibility, and storageability. Commercial table stock is still almost entirely hand graded.

Green Garlic—refers to freshly harvested bulbs that have not been fully cured and therefore weigh more than dried bulbs.

Green Manure—a crop grown specifically for its nutrient and raw organic matter content which is turned back into the soil while still lush and green (i.e., before they brown out and bolt or produce seed). Green manures are not harvested for food or hay; rather, they are used to feed the soil.

Greens (or "garlic greens")—the small, succulent, tender leaves of young garlic plants which are harvested once or twice in early spring for use as salad greens.

Habit—refers to the general appearance and manner of growth of a plant (i.e., the visual form of a plant).

Inflorescence—a cluster of flowers on a plant.

Italian Red (or Italian Purple)—a generic name that may be applied to almost any garlic whether or not it came from Italy or is red. At one time it was fairly synonymous in usage with the term "Artichoke," but its broad and often erroneous application has made the term nearly meaningless despite its continued popularity.

Leaf Angle—the angle at which the upper leaf blades grow away from the false stem of the plant. Varying leaf angles are part of the distinct growth habits of different varieties of garlic and are often described as upright, moderately spreading, spreading, or wide spreading in garlic.

Leaf Color—most garlic varieties have fairly distinctive ranges of leaf color, but colors can also be strongly affected by soil nutrients, temperatures, diseases, and insect attack. Garlic leaf colors are commonly called pale green, yellow-green, average green, deep green, or blue-green.

Longicuspis—literally "long cusp;" a species of wild ancestral garlic believed to be the progenitor of all cultivated garlic. The "long cusp" refers to the tall, pollen-bearing anthers which project visibly above the sepals and petals of the flowers. *A. longicuspis* is endemic to south central Asia.

Long Term Storage—the holding of garlic bulbs beyond their normal period of rest and through an enforced period of additional rest that is maintained by modifications in temperature, humidity, and air circulation. Six months of storage is "long term" for most ophio garlics but not for most Artichoke and Silverskin garlics.

Maturity—the point at which the maturation process is complete and bulbs are still in excellent condition with no deterioration.

Maturation Process—a period of time whose onset is signalled by the appearance of the flower stalk in ophio garlics and with the cessation of vegetative growth in all garlics. During the maturation process, plant leaves yellow and brown as they die back, to some extent because nutrients are being transferred from the foliage to the bulbs. Hard, lignified cloves skins are formed as well as dry outer bulb wrappers. Aerial bulbils may mature somewhat later than the below ground bulb. Garlic bulbs mature even if harvested a month before the occurrence of natural maturity in the soil. Most growers harvest bulbs before full maturity, at a point when approximately 60% of the foliage leaves are still green.

Mediterranean—the common name of an eco-geographic group of garlics identified by Komissarov as having evolved primarily in the region of the Caucasus, Turkey and the Near East, the Balkan states, the Crimea, and possibly the southern Ukraine. I suspect this term may be synonymous with "Rocambole" in the type of garlics it encompasses. Mediterranean may also refer to the broad climatic region of the above mentioned nations and regions, especially where summers are droughty and winter cold is well moderated by the influence of large bodies of water.

Micro Sprinkler—a low volume, low pressure sprinkler head that may be used for seed germination, crop irrigation, frost protection, or evaporative cooling.

Mold—any fungus that forms interwoven fibers (known as mycelium) on the surface of its structure. All fungi form molds, but in many the mold is not visible to the naked eye.

Neck—the portion of the plant adjacent to and directly above the bulb.

Node—the joints on the true stem from which garlic leaves arise, but also the joints where the upper leaf blades bend away from the lower leaf sheaths along the false stem.

Ophio Garlic—the term used by the author to denote subspecies *ophioscorodon* (i.e. hardneck, bolting garlic that produces a flower stalk).

Ophioscorodon—the botanical Latin name of the garlic subspecies that produces a woody flower stalk.

Origin—usually the country or region from which a named garlic strain came directly to America. Also often refers to the country or region (geographic or climatic) that a type of garlic evolved its current character in.

Partial Bolting—the process of forming a very short flower stalk that doesn't grow above the top foliage leaf and, therefore, produces the inflorescence and bulbils out the side of the false stem. In some cases the bulbils are even produced inside the bulb on top of the cloves. The flower stalk usually turns woody beneath the bulbils (as it does in ophioscorodon garlics) but no topsets are formed. Partial bolters are often variable from year to year; they may produce no bulbils, a few bulbils low in the stem, or occasionally even true topsets.

PI XXXXX—a "plant introduction" number assigned by the United States Department of Agriculture to newly imported plants. Other countries have other codes; for instance, the genebank at Bari, Italy, assigns an "MG" number.

Pekinense (or "pekinensis")—the species name originally applied by Prokhanov (1930) to a distinct Asian ophio garlic which Makino later determined to be only a variety. The author has not yet confirmed the existence of this variety, nor have modern researchers and professionals. (See book by Jones in bibliography.)

Period of Rest—technically, garlic bulbs do not experience true dormancy, but they do spend time in a "period of rest" which gradually decreases in depth and intensity in direct relation to storage temperatures. Rest is said to be completed when elongation of the sprout leaf begins inside the clove; however, new foliage leaves may be formed inside the clove and root nodules may begin to swell before rest is completed. Different varieties and strains of garlic have varying lengths of natural rest that correspond fairly well to the length of storage that is possible.

Photoperiodicity—the technical term for "day length sensitivity."

Plant Classification—an orderly, ranked system that divides plants into groups based on similarities, with each group becoming more exclusive as the group characteristics become more specific. Most people recognize the rankings of Family, Genus, and Species. Further subdivisions (in order) include subspecies, variety, horticultural group (or clone or cultivar or cultigen), and finally, strain.

Plicare—the Latin meaning is soft and pliable; suggested by the author to describe the variety of garlic commonly called Silverskin which rarely produces any bulbils in most climates and nearly always has a softneck.

Popping Tops—a phrase meaning "the act of breaking or cutting off the flower stalk of ophio garlics just above the top foliage leaf." The purpose is to increase bulb size by diverting energy away from bulbil production.

Quarantine—the isolation and protection of a commercial Allium producing area, state, or nation by the exclusion of all imported Alliums (particularly planting stock)that have not been inspected and declared free of serious diseases and insect pests. Most nations and some states require phytosanitary certificates declaring Alliums are free of white rot and stem and bulb nematode.

Quick Drop Knot—a knot commonly used to hang garlic bundles so that they may be quickly and easily removed. It is made from a loop of twine whose two loose ends are held together as one, then drawn around a hook or wire, and back over the top of themselves. Then, reach the thumb and forefinger through the loop, grab the two pieces as close as possible to the point where they cross over themselves and pull them towards you through the loop. The first loop will tighten up around the newly formed loop in your finger while the two loose ends remain free. The entire knot comes undone by pulling the two loose ends.

Red Garlic (or sometimes "rosy garlic")—a generic term usually referring to ophioscorodon garlics, but it is a confusing term since nearly all garlic strains have some bulbs with either reddish clove skins or purplish markings on the bulb wrappers. In addition, ophio garlics may have almost no red color in either the bulb skin or clove skin if grown in highly fertile soil. Varying degrees of challenge or stress (i.e. tight soils, reduced water or nutrients) seem to enhance color.

Rocambole—a particular group of ophio garlics (described by me as a distinct variety) in which the young succulent flower stalk forms from one to three tight 360 degree coils with the spathe and beak pointing straight up shortly after the stalk forms. As the garlic matures, the stalk loses its coil and stands up straight as it turns woody. All ophio garlics form stalks but non-Rocamboles have loose curls, three-fourths curls, or broad sweeping curves rather than tight coils.

Rotation (i.e., "crop rotation")—the changing of annual crops in any one field or location to plants of different families each year so that host specific insects and diseases cannot find a food source for more than one year at a time. Three to five year rotations (i.e., minimum three years between similar crops) are common for garlic and onion family crops. Rotations may also be used to vary soil nutrient demands and enhance soil organic matter levels by growing green manure crops.

Round—a small bulb that does not attain enough size to separate into individual cloves. Small cloves and bulbils often produce rounds the first year. Rounds generally have more vigor than cloves of the same size and will produce normal bulbs if planted. Elephant garlic may produce very large rounds.

Sativum—from the Latin meaning "cultivated," or literally "domesticated" (i.e., "not wild"). *Sativum* is the Allium species to which all cultivated garlics belong; it is also a subspecies of cultivated garlic (the double "*sativum*" meaning literally "highly domesticated") in which flower stalks are not normally formed, although in some types a short partial stalk is produced in which the flower cluster and bulbils appear as a swelling out the side of the false stem. Subspecies *sativum* bulbs usually consist of three or more clove layers in a whorl, though they sometimes occur in ophio fashion if a partial flower stalk is formed.

Scape—commonly called the "flower stalk;" technically, an "elongated internode." It rises from the true stem (below ground level), and its appearance signals the end of normal vegetative (leaf) growth. Scape growth commonly begins two to three weeks before the scape actually becomes visible above the top foliage leaf. The scape is often erroneously called a "seedstalk," but garlic produces only infertile flowers and no true seed.

Seedbulb—a technically incorrect term which is nonetheless commonly used when referring to garlic bulbs selected for use as planting stock.

Seedclove—a technically incorrect term which is commonly used when referring to individual garlic cloves intended for planting.

Seedstock—a misnomer often used instead of the correct term "planting stock" for garlic bulbs or cloves intended for planting. Planting stock is generally composed of large to very large bulbs from the healthiest plants which are free of disease, insects and damage, and which are sometimes left in the ground longer than table stock so that slight bulb blossoming occurs and individual cloves can be more easily separated from the bulb.

Selenium—rare, non-metallic, chemical element often found in association with sulphur ores, but also found in several allotropic forms which differ in physical and chemical properties but not in the basic atoms that compose it; ozone is an allotropic form of oxygen. In some forms selenium is biologically active and reported to affect fat levels, blood pressure, and the aging process in humans. Garlic is a selenium accumulator as are most brassicas and some other plants.

Semisagittalus—from the Latin "semi" meaning partial and "sagittalus" meaning arrow-like. The term was invented by the author to describe Artichoke garlics which have a strong tendency in many climates to bolt only partially. See "partial bolt."

Sheath (or "leaf sheath")—in garlic, the lower part of the foliage leaf which is wrapped around other leaf sheaths to form the false stem. A sheath can be any hardened or semi-hardened plant part that wraps around or encloses another plant part (e.g., the spathe is also a kind of sheath). The clove skins are a kind of sheath that are actually composed of leaf sheaths.

Size Grade—generally a one-half inch or one-quarter inch increment of measure used to describe either the minimum or maximum bulb diameter as measured horizontally from side to side (rather than end to end). Many small growers measure bulb diameter at the widest point and grade in one-half inch increments with 1.5 inches as the minimum size acceptable for table stock. The corresponding sizes might be called Large, Extra Large, and Premium. Others use one-quarter inch grade sizes. Colossal and Super Colossal are two of the size grades used in California. International and national standards seldom have different size grades; instead, they simply require a minimum bulb size.

Spathe—a large, sheath-like bract surrounding and enclosing the flower cluster and bulbils in a capsule that has an elongated beak. The spathe falls off most alliums at maturity but generally splits open and remains attached on garlic.

Spear (i.e. garlic spear)—the immature (young and succulent) umbel and spathe at the tip of a recently emerged flower stalk on ophio garlics. Spears can be removed shortly after they appear and sold as a gourmet vegetable.

Species—a group of plants with very similar character and, probably, a common ancestor. All cultivated garlic is the species *sativum* in the genus *Allium*.

Split Bulb—a term most commonly applied to overmature bulbs whose cloves have begun pushing away from the bulb center (in the general manner of a blooming flower) to the extent that bulb wrappers at the neck have been broken and the cloves inside the bulb are readily visible. The term may also refer to bulbs cracked open at the base from too much water or from insect and disease damage.

Split Skin—broken or cracked bulb wrappers that reveal the cloves, or broken or cracked clove skins that reveal the fleshy clove. Split skins are distinct from split bulbs although split bulbs always have split skins.

Spring Nonbolting—generally synonymous with "nonbolting." It refers to garlics that do not bolt in the spring (i.e., subspecies *sativum* or softneck garlics) and probably does not refer specifically to spring planted garlics that fail to bolt.

Stained Skins—bulb wrappers discolored and deteriorated in visible appearance by water or soil or soil micro-organisms.

Stem—see "**True Stem**" and "**False Stem**."

Strain—the lowest subdivision of plant classification usually representing slight variations between members of the same variety. "Strain" is often used interchangeably with cultivar, but cultivars are, usually of hybrid origin. "Strain" can also be interchangeable with "cultigen" which is a varietal variation of unknown origin. "Spanish Roja" and "Russian Red" are examples of named strains of garlic that are both within variety Rocambole.

Stunted—garlic plants of smaller than normal size due to reduced growth caused by disease, insects, water or nutrient deficiencies.

Subspecies—today, virtually interchangeable with "variety," but in the strictest sense, more inclusive (broader) than a variety. Subspecies is often used to denote a geographical variant of a species, or a variation in flower color, leaf size, etc. The author uses the term to distinguish between bolting and nonbolting garlics. The Latin "sub" means almost or not quite (i.e., not quite a species).

Table Stock—fully cured and dried bulbs intended for marketing and human consumption rather than for processing or planting. Table stock is generally of top quality, and very uniform and attractive in appearance.

Thin Skins—refers generally to dried garlic bulbs which have only one or two remaining bulb wrappers especially when the inner cloves can be seen through the skins. It may also refer to the actual thickness of the individual bulb wrappers, which tend to be thinner and more brittle when grown in clay soil or tight soils very low in organic matter, tilth, and texture.

Topset—a flower cluster at the top of a flower stalk produced by ophio garlics and eventually including aerial bulbils in a beaked spathe.

Topsetter—any garlic that produces topsets.

Trait—plant, bulb, and clove tendencies that are inherited but also variable, sometimes over a wide range, due to environmental influences such as soil, climate, day length, etc.

True Stem—the main stalk of a plant supporting leaves and flowers. In garlic the true stem is extremely short (nearly flat) and entirely below ground at the base of the bulb or at the point between roots and leaves. The above ground portion of the plant that appears as a stem is known as a "false stem."

Twisted Leaves—grossly misshapen foliage leaves on growing plants; often occurs in association with stunting (and for the same basic reasons). Twisted leaves may involve contortion, or a spiraling, whorlish pattern of growth.

Umbel—in garlic the term usually refers to the entire topset at the tip of the flower stalk, including spathe and beak, flowers, and bulbils.

Variety—modification within a species; the term is technically more specific (i.e., more exclusive) than "subspecies." The term is commonly applied to named garlic strains, but I believe the term is better applied to four or five specific types of garlic whose descriptive characters are more specific than at the subspecies level but less specific than at the level of individual named strains.

White Garlic—a generic term usually referring to softneck garlics of the sativum subspecies (i.e., Artichoke or Silverskin varieties), but a confusing term since many of these garlics have reddish clove skins and red-purple markings on the bulb wrappers. See also "Red Garlic."

White Rot—a serious fungal disease of garlic and other Alliums. There are no direct controls, and the fungus may persist in soils more than ten years after alliums are no longer grown.

Wild Garlic—naturally evolved garlic that has not been tended, selected, or domesticated by people. There are many species of wild garlic in the world. The most famous is perhaps *Allium longicuspis*. Wild Ransom's Garlic is a well know potherb. In the U.S.A., *Allium veneale* (or "field garlic) is a well known weed. Many wild garlics were collected and used as food by native Amerindian cultures.

Winter Bolting—any garlic that is typically planted in the fall and which forms a flower stalk in late spring.

Index